# POWER
# AUTHORITY
# DOMINION

## A LIFETIME OPPORTUNITY FOR ALL

*Includes a simple but powerful and beneficial
Mental Health Activity at the end.*

NAOMIE PRAISE

United Kingdom

# CONTENTS

# 1
## THE DEPTHS OF DOMINION

There are four different words for dominion in the Hebrew language but one of them is radah, which means to rule or to takeover. Dominion is sovereignty or control. It's also an act of supremacy and ascendancy or superiority. In other words, it's defined as a man's attempt to establish dominion over nature. However, many of us today, have chosen to misuse dominion and act negatively about it. One thing we need to understand is that there's a positive and negative side of dominion, but several have chosen to follow the negative side. Dominion works with faith for it to manifest in our lives. This is an opportunity for all to receive dominion, power and authority through Jesus Christ and nowhere or anyone else. God gave us the dominion over sin once we stand against it.

We can dominate anything that's trying to pull us down if we have Christ in us. A perfect example of dominion is an eagle, because they teach us to stay present, patient and to constantly fix our eyes to the future, but still remember of our present environment. Eagles can dominate in a positive way but can also attack when they see danger. Eagles don't allow anything takeover them, they will not let you bully them. Eagles have the character of leadership and to have this you need to have dominance in you. They have a strong vision, the capacity to see the reality and make accurate predictions as to what's happening from afar distance. A person who carries dominion, can takeover, just like eagles, they are very fearless. They defend themselves when a storm comes using their wings, to soar to greater heights. Eagles take benefits of the storm that smaller birds fear and run away from.

When eagles fly, you can easily see how bold and clear their eyes are watching for its prey. It's important to grab an opportunity when you first see it and act immediately. This is what an eagle does, they waste no time, especially if they know it's for their own benefit, they will activate, the power, authority and the dominion they have, to take the opportunity. Therefore, if you want to take dominion in a positive way, have the character of an eagle and you will always go higher then whatever is trying to scare you.

In Psalm 8:6 it says, "Behold, I have given him dominion over the works of your hands; you have put all things under his feet". This is a lifetime opportunity for all, meaning that anyone can get to this point if they are willing.

# 2

# THE DEPTHS OF POWER

The word power means the ability to control people and events. It's also a way of accomplishing something. One of the Hebrew words for 'power' is *Ozaz*, which is found in Psalms 90:11, "If only we knew the power of your anger! Your wrath is as great as the fear that is your due. Teach us to number our days, that we may gain a heart of wisdom." This shows that we need to use our capacities well and on time because there's power in life. When you don't know how to number your days, you will be drained on useless things. You need to have faith to live in power. To have power, you need to discover it first. You need to be willing to know the power you possess. The only power that is legitimate is God's very own. Any other power out of God's will is not legitimate. I'm referring to evil, demonic powers they don't last because a time will come where you will be exposed. God's power is authentic and true.

We have the power to change things through wisdom. It's like losing your life because you were careless and refused to use the power you have, to fight for your life. When an individual has power, it means they have control over things and people. Power also means influence, so it's important to know the power of your desire in terms of your intimacy for God and the people you love. Cindy Trimm said "You should never give your personal power, during a crisis". That's why it's important to establish healthy boundaries, to protect your power as an individual.

In the New Testament, power is used so many times in different stories and it is used to describe the unseen world. Jesus practiced power over the unseen world through his exorcism of demons, which is found In Mark 6:7 "Calling the Twelve to him, he began to send them out two by two and gave them authority over impure spirits." This shows how we can use our powers as Children of God. Apostle Paul lived an empowerment life after he had an encounter with Jesus. He was filled with power even in his words and now we are influenced and inspired by his teachings. The reason, he was able to become Paul, instead of remaining Saul was because the power of sin came out of him, then the power of God located him for an eternal change. Exodus 7:8-13 says, "Then the LORD told Moses and Aaron, "When Pharaoh says to you, 'Perform a miraculous sign,' then you are to say to Aaron, 'Take your staff and throw it in front of Pharaoh.' It will become a serpent." So, Moses and Aaron went into Pharaoh and did what the LORD had commanded them. Aaron threw his staff in front of Pharaoh and his officials, and it became a serpent. Then Pharaoh also called for the wise men and sorcerers, and they—along with the Egyptian magicians—did the same thing with their secret arts. So, each one threw down his staff and it became a serpent, but Aaron's staff swallowed up their staffs. Yet Pharaoh's heart was stubborn, and he did not listen to them, just as the LORD had said would happen." This scripture is clearly demonstrating the power of God, through a simple staff that anyone can gain a lifetime opportunity to hold but the fact that Moses had God in him, that's how power was revealed and released. There must be a power from you to heal nations. God used Moses' staff to show people how powerful he can make us who accept to receive a lifetime opportunity. His staff became a snake and completed many other missions to prove Pharaoh, along with the magicians wrong. I want us to understand God is the one who gives the real power and magicians are copycats just like their father the devil.

When you discuss about power in a spiritual sense, we can see it represents the Christian life, an empowerment that comes from

God almighty. In 2 Peter 1:3 it says," his divine power has given us everything we need for life and godliness." So, this is an opportunity of a lifetime for all, especially those who are born again. I need you to understand that there's power in you as a human and a child of God. However, the devil tries to make you feel powerless when you are persecuted. God's power is divine, meaning that it's pure and truthful. This is not passive but to inspire us in every way possible, so we don't get carried away with discouragement.

# 3

# THE DEPTHS OF AUTHORITY

One of the Hebrew words for authority is *tokef*, which means power, strength and energy. Authority is like dominion and power because they all have influence over people. Authority is the decent or permissible right or aptitude to control. It is the right to command, to have a strong opinion that attracts others to you. The type of group that has authority and can command with full force, is the government. This is because the president confirms what the government says, and this is what I called a dictating authority. Authority also works along with faith, for it to be effective in our lives.

Dominion, power, and authority are all superior orders. So, when we put dominion, power and authority together, we should understand that the word, dominion, transmits with it, an awareness of territory. It is the law, which gives authority. Power is devoted in ambassadors. God gave us the opportunity to rule His creation by shaping, developing, and exploring different things he has created and use it to dominate for His glory. This kind of authority is a very powerful notion, that is occupied with probable and risks.

When you read the bible, you will see that many have abused the kind of authority God gave us by maltreating others. The kind of authority God has given to us, is a vital one, for the kingdom of God. Jesus himself took the opportunity to practice authority in His own ministry. As it is mentioned in Mark 3:7-11 Whenever the impure spirits saw him, they fell before him and cried out, "You are the Son of God." But he gave them strict orders not to tell others about him. " He also demonstrated authority over demons and diseases in (Mark 3:15). As human beings, you don't have to tear, manipulate, kill, or negatively control people to take dominion. Power and authority shouldn't make you desire to destroy others in order dominate. But you also need power, authority and determination in order to take dominion. When you have power and authority, people will obey you because of the influence you have on them. This is also called dominion. But ensure you have the authority and power from God and not from the devil.

The Christian Bible (King James Version) mentions in Genesis 1:26-28 "And God said, Let us make man in our image, after our likeness: and let them have dominion over the fish of the sea, and over the fowl of the air, and over the cattle, and over all the earth, and over every creeping thing that creepeth upon the earth. So, God created man in his own image, in the image of God created he him; male and female created he them." God meant for us to be a blessing to the earth and everything in it including animals, when he said, "Have dominion over..." God's intention was not to hurt innocent people or animals, neither to control, dominate others in a wrong way. This also meant that God has given us a lifetime opportunity to dominate over everything on earth.

Now, that's what I consider as real power and authority because it's authentic. I've also identified that God did not say animals can have dominion, but he allowed man to have dominion over everything, that included animals as well. You will notice that God did not just give man dominion, (so people in general) but he also gave couples their own type dominion, power, and authority when it came to their marriages.

I strongly believe that God's desire was for us to stand our ground, stay firm and be a blessing to others on earth. But His will for us, is not to take advantage of people around us by having dominion over them negatively. It's very possible to rule and control positively because everything is possible to God and there's hope for every living.

An example of a woman who really exercised her authority with full power and dominion given to her by God, was Esther.

Although she was an orphan, it didn't stop her from doing what was right for the Jews. She wrote the letters with not some but all authority, as she was not only a child of God but a Queen. So, we can see how she prevailed, used her power and dominion in a positive way, to be a blessing and change lives of her people, which is found in Esther 9:29. Esther's influence of power, authority and dominion, also encouraged, inspired and empowered the Jewish people to stand up for their rights.

This shows that, as a population, they multiplied and became great because of one person's decision of taking the opportunity of a lifetime. The scriptures say, "After this I looked, and there before me was a great multitude that no one could count, from every nation, tribe, people and language, standing before the throne and before the Lamb" Revelation 7: 4-9. Esther practiced the right domination by helping her nation. She carried excessive favour of God and that's how she conquered. Esther received this authority by being the queen to her husband who was the king. Despite her history, she was a kind and understanding soul that had authority and power as a woman in those days. She had to use and hold onto the weapon of power to proceed with her plans. She had some characteristics of an eagle, even as a woman of her generation. Esther was fierce, strong at heart, wise in mind and made a difference and never ran away from the storm but faced it, just like an eagle. A person who carries power, authority and dominion doesn't talk to too much. They have their heads down most of the time, in focusing to think, reflecting, planning, and praying before they could raise their heads up to proceed in wisdom.

The bible says in Proverbs 29:2 "When the righteous are in authority the people rejoice but when a wicked person rules, the people groan." This means we have everlasting authority as children of God. This scripture also tells us that a person who is living right and using their dominion, authority and power correctly is a blessing to people because they will bring joy and peace. But a person who is not righteous before God will always bring wickedness and that's a best friend of darkness. There will be no peace, no joy, and no stability when such person is around. A wicked heart will destroy anything good that was built before their leadership; this happens through wrong domination, power, and authority. If a wicked person gets power, dominion, and authority over others, they will treat people unfairly.

# 4

# O'CLOCK

Mahashaa is the modern Hebrew word for what time is it? Time is of the essence, so it's important to take a lifetime opportunity because its available to all. You need to know what you are doing with your time. We need to understand that time drags when we're bored even if the same period can fly by while watching a fascinating show. The same thing can happen in terms of time because it can last forever while reading a boring book. But when we're bored, we are extremely focused on ourselves. This can lead us to think too much, which can waste our time. Time slows when we face ambiguity, especially when we are sometimes not ready. But if we must wait 10 minutes in detention, then those same 10 minutes can appear agonizingly long. When we don't know what's coming up for us, we ponder on it much. This shows that time slows when we're waiting, but at times it could be for a good purpose.

When you hear this question what time it is? you may quickly say to me "Oh it's 12o'clock", which you could be right. What time is it? implies, if it's the right time to carry out an assignment, is it the time to start the business, job, ministry, have children or even to get married? You need to know the time you're in, this includes the end times, battle time, enjoying time, time to leave, time to enter, harvesting time, or reaping time. Many of us have struggled to discern the time we are in and the seasons, that's why we fuss and get into trouble a lot. Sometimes, you don't see the fruit the day you plant the seed. Remember everything is for an appointed time and the time isn't ready for what you have in store, and 'non' is really 'not now'. So, you're not being rejected but promoted but this doesn't mean you should waste your time in worthless things. Waiting upon the Lord is something we need to learn and master; despite the discouragement and disappointment the devil tries to throw at us.

David in the Bible, knew what time it was, he knew it was striking o'clock and not sleeping or pitying o'clock when Goliath came into the picture. Your time and every second of your life are vital, so what you do with it really matters. Remember, time waits for no one, so whenever time gives you the opportunity to use it, make sure you grab and produce something great out of the time. You need to also discover the appointed time, just like God remembered Sarah at the appointed time. I know it's very easy to be forcing things to happen, especially when we are fed up, tired and pressured but something will tell you that it's not time yet. I know that a time is coming where you recover every lifetime opportunity you lost in Jesus's name.

Everyone experiences time differently and time moves more quickly when we're older, that's the more reason we should grab every good opportunity to enjoy ourselves and achieve amazing things at its appoint time. Hannah knew what time it is when she was facing the hardest time of her life. She knows it was kneeling and roaring o'clock in prayer and not responding o'clock to Peninnah's pettiness. If you allow this, you will miss a lifetime opportunity to focus on better things. Knowing the time to fight and when to not will save you. You need to know that time is a mystery, and it exists, as you think about the power, dominion, and authority you possess. You need to also understand that the past and future are equally real. So, it is time to stop living in the past, so don't allow yourself to focus on the past pains. Whenever, there's an opportunity to enter the active mode, take the time do something before you forget, as your memory is it as good you think.

We are missing out on so many opportunities because we are either in the wrong place at the wrong time or we are not managing our times correctly. Dr Juanita Bynum said on one her Facebook live videos "When I get up in the morning, I will use that time to just dump it all, like placing things where they're supposed to be". Dr Juanita Bynum also added by saying, "Because if you do not, you will wake up with thoughts being misplaced." So, she discovered what time it is in her life, it was time for her to place things where it supposes to be. This also means to dump every negativity and emotional breakdowns; otherwise, it will steal your valuable time. At night-time, you need to do a recall, in the morning time start at fresh and allow new opportunities to step in your life. Exodus 9:5 The Lord set a definite time, saying, "Tomorrow the Lord will do this thing in the land." Maybe today is not the time for what you planned, but God says it's tomorrow. I went through seasons where I'm pressured and want to do things so quickly because of pressure, frustration, and tiredness. However, I didn't realise that it was God's time for to me to release my project to the world. Later, I understood that God still wanted me to pour in more out of my heart before I can fully be ready. At times the clock is not ticking but we want to get it ticking by force. This means, get working and allow preparation in the secret, until the clock ticks for you to expand. Therefore, we end up hurting innocent souls, marrying wrong, going to wrong places, and making decisions out of anger.

# 5

# THE POWER OF SACRED GARMENTS

The ability to wear a scared garment is a whole gift, not given to everyone. This means that you must be selected, chosen, called and different because sacred garments carry great power. You can't be like everyone else and expect the grace to wear a sacred garment. You can't live a normal life or be a normal human being if you're required to wear a sacred garment. Wearing a sacred garment can also be undeserving but it is a favour from God. It is like a uniform and a unique apparel and sanctified in the blood of Jesus. To take dominion, power and authority, you must wear a sacred garment, that even if anyone attempts to steal it from you, it will not work on them but only on you. It is like wearing a strong soldier uniform, that protects even from bullets, it will look magical but it's a reality. This can be an opportunity of a lifetime for all but only those who make efforts and understands the assignment will wear the sacred garment. Hence why I said it's not given to everyone so easily.

There's always a reason for a scared garment being made to be worn. It doesn't stay on display for no reason. It's not worn all the time but occasionally and when required to. A sacred garment is not to be taken for granted. In Exodus 28 says "Have Aaron your brother brought to you from among the Israelites, along with his sons Nadab and Abihu, Eleazar and Ithamar, so they may serve me as priests.

Make sacred garments for your brother Aaron to give him dignity and honour. Tell all the skilled workers to whom I have given wisdom in such matters that they are to make garments for Aaron, for his consecration, so he may serve me as priest". Therefore, we can see that the sacred garment was to give them dignity and honour that lasts. It becomes like your identity because that's what people will see in you. One thing we can capture here is the fact that God sent a specific person to cloth them with the sacred garment. Therefore, we need to ask God to send us skilled people who will cloth us with our sacred garment. Notice that those who was chosen to make those sacred garments, were skilled to do so. This means that It had to be specific people and not just anyone to take on the role. These people who are to cloth you with sacred garments are considered as destiny helpers because they contributed to your elevation. To be skilled, means to be in alignment, focused, empowered, equipped to do the task. Be careful who you allow to cloth you because many people have an evil heart and may curse or inflict a disease on your sacred garment. A person that wears a sacred garment is already walking in glory, power, dominion and authority. Hence when they speak, people listen and obey them. That's the power of a sacred garment.

When I began secondary school, I remember being addressed as "You are not normal, you're so weird", other pupils would run away from me because I was telling them about Jesus and advising them to stop doing bad things. At that young age, I didn't really understand what the love of God was, but I knew God loved us all and wanted us to run away from sin. I was not really the kind of pupil in secondary that had friends or people crowding me because I didn't fit in with what they did. I also never knew that God wanted us His children to be different from everyone else. Being different is like you've been given another garment that is sacred, pure and not easily ripped. It will have to take a lot for it to be destroyed. When you become a child of God, you receive, the power, dominion and authority to be different. This means a child of God is no longer a normal being, you've become a spirit being. A child of God should never see themselves as a human being but a spirit being because the bible says there must be a difference between those who serve me and those who don't. Children of God are not normal and are extraordinary. To be a child of God is a lifetime opportunity that anyone is free to receive. The essence of not being normal, is an opportunity for all but you need to add spices like dominion, authority and power because you are no longer seen as a human being but a spirit being. Therefore, a person who is required to wear a scared garment is no longer considered as a normal person but an extraordinary person and different because you will have a lifetime opportunity to obtain dominion, power and authority under this pure clothing. However, you need to maintain a prayer life to be able to keep the sacred garment as a lifetime opportunity.

Moreover, this scripture, shows us how importance of a sacred garment is in our lives. In Exodus 28 verse 43 it says, "Aaron and his sons must wear them whenever they enter the tent of meeting or approach the altar to minister in the Holy Place, so that they will not incur guilt and die". God wants us to understand that sacred garments is also a cloth of protection and can't be used anyhow. This implies that you can't be clubbing, prostituting, stealing or doing all kinds of evil and wear a sacred garment at the same time. A scared garment is not for people who conduct like this. However, you can be amongst the chosen and it can be a lifetime opportunity for anyone who turns away from their evil ways and lives a righteousness life. Just like Noah, who was righteous and blameless in God's sight and the Lord remembered him and those around him.

A sacred garment can be earned or inherited, in other words, it can be passed on to other generations because it's like a mantel. On the other hand, many are wearing garments of shame and not sacred ones. Your garment of shame could be a certain sickness, failure, condemnation, lies, sexual immorality, masturbation, marital issues, stagnation, or demonic resistances. As you read this, I command all these garments of shame in your life to be stripped off and burnt by the fire of the Holy Ghost, in Jesus's name. In 2021, I conducted a woman retreat event that consisted of deliverance and healing against garments of shame. The power of God was really manifesting, and people were delivered and testified.

# 6

## GUILT THE SILENT KILLER

Guilt is a feeling of being unhappy or worried about something you have done wrong, in the past or present. An example of this, could be hurting another person and their presence making you feel uncomfortable. You cannot take dominion if you carry guilt in you, because you will keep making unnecessary mistakes that could trigger those around you. Guilt can isolate and make you lose your appetite. Guilt makes you pretend around those you've hurt and that will make you lose your power, authority and the individual dominion you had. Maybe the person who might of have had a high level of respect for you, but ever since, you've been acting weird and pretending around them, they've realised, that you are hiding something bad you have done to them.

As a result, they will disrespect and disregard you. You won't be able to live with people freely because of guilt. Guilt will destroy any other relationships you've built because you can't hide it for too long. It will come to light one day, as your frustrations, fear and confusions pile up, each time you think about it. Then it will explode and show up. The Bible says in Luke 8:17 "For there is nothing hidden that will not be disclosed, and nothing concealed that will not be known or brought out into the open". This tells us that, you can run but you can't hide forever. Proverbs 11:12 says "The wicked will not go unpunished, but those who are righteous will go free". This means your guilt is killing you slowly because you are being punished for it consciously physically and spiritually. Guilt keeps you living in the past and that shouldn't be your portion. You need to rebuke the guilt, confess, and live right. Don't allow yourself to continue living with that guilt.

One thing that I know, is that we are being observed by someone out there, so one way or the other, people will discover your guilt. The longer you hold unto the guilt, the more it will mess with your head. In order, to avoid guilt from occurring, apologise immediately to the person you've hurt, whenever an opportunity of a lifetime comes. Then, pray and ask God to forgive you, so you can be at peace.

I watched a Nigerian movie, that showed how a married woman was misled by a friend to poison her husband's food. She tried but the chef worker in the house caught her and warned her boss not to eat the food. Then the husband decided to send her wife back to her parent's house, because the act was very serious. A few weeks later, the husband decided to bring her wife back to their matrimonial home, but the wife kept on refusing. This was because she felt so guilty of what she tried to do to her husband. She was scared and couldn't trust herself anymore to cook for the husband, knowing that he might not eat her food. She was guilty and kept on blaming herself, whether her husband will sleep calmly around her, knowing very well of the past negative domination she had on him.

But at the end, the husband convinced her as he still trusted her, then she came back home after learning to forgive and trust herself. She could have destroyed her home and life completely if she continued to allow guilt to dominate her. So, we see how guilt can damage and negatively dominate someone's life gradually. Guilt makes you believe that you can't have a second chance, you can't fix it again and that you can't be a better person. But that's all lies from the devil, as there's hope for tomorrow.

# 7

# THE POWER OF WISDOM

To dominate, you need the wisdom components because people will desire to work with wise people. Wisdom is a gift provided by God himself, for free of charge. Just like eagles, they have great wisdom and can visualise from afar. Eagles are wise enough to know what's likely to happen because of their sharp eyes. God made them so unique and extremely different from all the other animals. They possess power that can allow them dominate animals who live on the ground, but in a good way. Therefore, it's important to have eyes like an eagle, to exercise the dominion, authority, and power that God gave you and to use them with wisdom.

Many people were born wise, and some prayed for it. But a man in the Bible was favoured by God to receive wisdom, despite being a King. I will have you know that not all kings are wise. I've never heard of a poor king and if he was not wise, he will always be surrounded by wise cabinet workers in the kingdom that would help him. The bible says in 1Kings 3:1-15 "The king went to Gibeon to offer sacrifices, for that was the most important high place, and Solomon offered a thousand burnt offerings on that altar. At Gibeon the LORD appeared to Solomon during the night in a dream, and God said, "Ask for whatever you want me to give you."

Even though, Solomon asked God for wisdom, but I want us to catch the revelation in this dream encounter, and this was the offering he offered on the altar. The revelation in this, is the word 'trigger', and this is because God saw his offering and it triggered Him to visit Solomon in his dreams. Not only that, but Solomon's good act led to God favouring him to ask for anything and it will be given to him. In saying this, I am encouraging you to learn and know what triggers God either positively or negatively. Some people always look at the word triggering in such a negative way. But you will probably be astonished to hear, that a trigger can be in a good or bad way.

For example, offerings and tithes triggers God to bless us, so this is a positive sense of triggering, which brings us to a positive way of dominion, power, and authority. Therefore, it is important to have an offering heart, so you can dominate positively. Solomon was not aware that God will visit him but surprisingly, He did, and it was for a good purpose, which transformed Solomon's life. This could be an opportunity of a lifetime for all, but only if we understand this concept and revelation, then anyone can receive this opportunity. Solomon asked for the inner spirit, which is the Holy Spirit. Wisdom and knowledge are symbols of the Holy Spirit. This means that God is watching our actions, just like he saw Solomon's and appeared to him in his dreams. If you have wisdom, you can also trigger beautiful things to come your way positively. This leads to positive domination because people will love to be around someone who is wise. The bible says in 1Kings 3:1-15, Solomon made an alliance with Pharaoh king of Egypt and married his daughter. He brought her to the City of David until he finished building his palace and the temple of the LORD, and the wall around Jerusalem. The people, however, were still sacrificing at the high places, because a temple had not yet been built for the Name of the LORD. Solomon showed his love for the LORD by walking according to the instructions given him by his father David, except that he offered sacrifices and burned incense on the high places. Solomon answered, "You have shown great kindness to your servant, my father David, because he was faithful to you and righteous and up upright in heart. You have continued this great kindness to him and have given him a son to sit on his throne this very day".

Apart from the grace God gave Solomon to receive wisdom, God had a powerful relationship with his father David. We can say that David was a man full of wisdom by the way he lived. He was quick to repent when he fell into temptation, that's one of the reasons why God called David a man according to my heart.

This wisdom was because he knew how to amend things with God and his people. David used wisdom to fight goliath by acquiring for God's assistance. He was also powerful a prophet of God that was loved by his people, after they saw all that God performed in his life. This shows that David dominated positively many times, whilst he was alive. He grabbed an opportunity of a lifetime that could be given to anyone that asks for it. So, we see the traits of David in his son, as God was also with Solomon. In addition, I could say that wisdom ran in David's family because it started with him and then landed to his son Solomon.

Wisdom was like a heritage for Solomon, due to the acts his father did that brought many blessings to them. Wisdom can save you from many troubles because it will help you make the right decisions. Wisdom can save you from using incorrect words and phrases when speaking to someone about a sensitive topic. Wisdom allows you to do important things that matter, it won't allow you to waste time. We can see in many ways, that God favoured Solomon because of his father's faithfulness.

So, it means that our children's can benefit from our faithfulness and righteousness towards God. Domination can be generational but it's up to us to choose whether, it will be in a positive way or not. To decide this, it will require wisdom and you can get it, if you ask God, just like Solomon did. This links to parables, because in the bible parables causes us to understand things beyond the physical, which can be considered as an element of wisdom. To dominate you need the spirit of understanding and wisdom. To understand Jesus's language of parable speaking, you need to have the spirit of discernment, as deeper revelations await to be unfolded through those parables. Parables helps us to understand life in a better sense and beyond our imaginations.

We need to know that the Holy is our best friend, I've touched on more about him on my first book and how He has been good to me, through my personal life experiences. If God gives you the opportunity to ask anything, please ask for important and not silly things. You need to understand that God promises us the Holy Spirit through His Son Jesus Christ as he departed back to His Father. For scriptures says in John

14:25-26, "All this I have spoken while still with you. But the Advocate, the Holy Spirit, whom the Father will send in my name, will teach you all things and will remind you of everything I have said to you". In other words, the Holy Spirit can fill us with the spirit of wisdom for any assignment he has given to us.

# 8

# PAD: IN MARRIAGE, DIVORCED, SINGLE, ENGAGED

Dominance is also an important element of marriage. As a couple, you must have the power and authority to dominate, especially when it comes to marital attacks and setbacks. You gain a holy dominion through accepting Jesus Christ in your life, who is the way, truth, and life. It is wrong to use the dominion God gave you to mistreat your significant other. Rather, you can dominate in your marriage by overcoming people or things that fight to bring you both down. Marriage is not for babies or adults but for the mature in mind. When I speak of dominion, authority, and power in marriage I don't mean the act of controlling or confiscating your spouse's bank account, hiding things from your significant other and treating them as if they are nothing. This means to be transparent, loyal, trustworthy, respectful, kind and submissive. This is the right way of dominion because when your spouse sees your positive way of dominance, he will have no choice then to surprise you with beautiful things. In my marriage, we've had to take dominion over every person's negativity and words against us and destroyed them, through prayer. As result many people hated us because we refused to be used and wrongly dominated and overpowered by people.

Dominion will help you know and have confidence in who you are. In the Christian Bible it says in Genesis 1:28, "God blessed them and said to them, be fruitful and increase in number; fill the earth and subdue it. Rule over the fish in the sea and the birds in the sky and over every living creature that moves on the ground". In this scripture, I've come to understand that God's intention was for us to have dominion over everything on earth positively, but the devil has deceived many to have dominion over everything negatively. If as a couple, you don't have these components such as dominion, power and authority, you won't be able to overcome the battles that's in your marriage. As a single woman, you must take the opportunity to use the dominion, power and authority for God's glory. This means, dominating anything or anyone that wastes your time and makes you feel worthless. Don't full for the sweet-sour talk of the devil because he will steal the positive dominion, power and authority God placed in you. In addition, you should use the dominion, power and authority stored in you to overcome all temptations and not to simply give in. If you don't use the lifetime opportunity that God has given to you, which is to dominate, have power and authority, you won't be able to rule over the battles that awaits you in your future marital life. Whatever marital status you are in, take dominion by bettering yourself, so you can move forward.

# 9
## THE ART OF LOVE

It's crucial to have love in us above anything else, if we truly want to be effective and dominate correctly. This is the greatest commandment God gave us to practice and maintain. I conducted a virtual programme in the women ministry that I lead, known as Wife Let's Pray. On that programme I hosted, my guest emphasised on love, especially when working in the health care sector, as a Christian woman. We discovered that you cannot dominate without the heart of love. Love allows you to operate in the best of your ability, so that things are done well. When love is in your heart, there will be no room for hate, jealousy, or envy. But no matter how they are moving, you move with a pure heart, that's the art of love. Perfect love drives out fear, as a child of God.

A perfect example of love is Jesus Christ the Son of God, who left the throne to die for us on the cross. He was beaten, hated, accused, and treated in all manner of ways, but his love for God's people led him to stick with what was written in the scriptures, which is the will of the Father. This means, you must die to self, to love. Love never boasts but humbles an individual. Do you realise that it's very hard to show genuine love when you are angry or upset with someone? Well, I've been through it on several occasions and that made me lose opportunities of a lifetime to communicate and connect with my divine helpers. This is very bad because I was destroying myself unknowingly. If you agree with me, then you should understand the difficulty of practicing the art of love.

You must look beyond hate and consider the love of God and you will end up doing the right things for yourself and others. Love can lead you to the right people and right decisions in a difficult situation, that could have gotten you into trouble. Love has brought families to reconcile, after years of hate and killing each other, over worthless things. This reminds me of Joseph's life in the bible (Genesis 37). He is a perfect example of family reconciliation because his brothers plotted against him for sharing his dream with them. But put to shame when they discovered that he became great in Egypt. Furthermore, Joseph had the art of love in him, to move on and never hold a grudge against his brothers, for trying to use his dream against him.

On the other hand, you should sometimes learn to love people from afar, especially those who don't understand and are constantly hurting you. When Pharaoh, the king of Egypt accepted the children of Israel in his land, he didn't have the art of love in him for the people of Israel (Exodus 1). His motive was to make them slaves, maltreat them for as long as he wanted. He didn't obey the commandant of love that God gave us, and God didn't take it lightly with him. When you love conditionally and with a benefit of destroying someone at the end, you will be dealt with severely. Love is a performance that works with consistency, dedication, passion, and happiness, this equals an art of love. Love is an opportunity of a lifetime for all, but it must be nurtured. Love can be stubborn but ensure it is for the right reasons, that can lead to positive dominion, power, and authority, that also brings an opportunity of a lifetime.

Matthew 22:36-40, "Teacher, which is the greatest commandment in the Law?" Jesus replied: "Love the Lord your God with all your heart and with all your soul and with all your mind. This is the first and greatest commandment. And the second is like it: 'Love your neighbour as yourself. All the Law and the Prophets hang on these two commandments". In this scripture Jesus Christ clarifies and gives us a revelation that love is Himself because God is love. When Jesus says, "And the second is like it", he means that both commandments are very similar to each other. It also shows that He is the author of love, so either way, we are required to practice the first and the second to ourselves and to others. If the Prophets and the laws hanged on two these commandments, it means they understood the art of love and survived it in their time. Therefore, we can do the same in today's world. So, if you think you can't then, God would have never mentioned about it in the first place.

You will notice in this scripture, even if it's not directly mentioned, that Jesus didn't only indicate to practice one of the commandments, but both. The word greatest can also mean the most important, the top, the biggest above all. So, you can already imagine the importance of the art of love whilst looking at this scripture. This proves what the scriptures says that love is the greatest indeed because nothing good can be done without love, as love is also the act of sacrifice. Loving God with everything in you, without any argument or hesitations, is the art of love. This refers to your heart, mind and soul. So, don't take love as a joke. You see, the same way you get hurt in a relationship due to love and go through depression, anxiety, suicidal thoughts, and you don't expect anyone to take it as a joke; it's the same way you shouldn't take God as a joke because He is love. When you don't love God, it hurts Him that you are missing out on greatness because love is the greatest commandment of them all. If you know the importance of love and you don't practice it, you should be ashamed of yourself because you are depriving those who truly deserve it. Love is an opportunity of a lifetime for all, and everyone deserves to be loved at least once in their life; including the undeserved.

The second is like the first because God is telling us to love in so many ways, which will benefit every part of our bodies, minds, souls and hearts. This also implies that we should show our body, soul, mind and heart love as we practice loving God, by being positive and living a life that glorifies God. It is only the art of love that will lead you into beautiful things regardless of the pains you are enduring. This is done through Jesus Christ, the Son of God. Loving God is the act of loving His people, who are our neighbours, with all our hearts, that way we can be sure that we are loving God with all our hearts, souls, and minds. This means to care for our neighbours with sincerity. You can't be your brother or sister's keeper without having the art of love, no matter how rich or popular you are. Love will make you first, if you can love God with all your heart, soul and mind.

This is a duty for us to practice, which is to love God, ourselves, and others. If you can't love yourself, how can you show other's love? it will mean that you have no idea of the meaning of love, until you are taught by someone who knows the true meaning of love. Love is never perfect because love allows you to make a mistake but teaches you to change and move on, with a positive mindset. This includes not holding any grudges after getting hurt. Love is sometimes not fair because, it hurts the other person who doesn't see things the same way as you do. Now, you will have to suffer, simply because you love, and the others don't love like you do. But continue to love anyways, as you reap only what you sow.

Love is a very powerful tool, but it is not an absence of war in our lives. People may argue today but speak again the next minute because of love. Love brings peace to those who are troubled and lovely people deserve it too. Love helps you value your situation and treat everyone equally. Love allows you to forgive those who doesn't even deserve your forgiveness. Love is equal, love is also justice because it never allows the innocent to suffer in eyes of the law, especially if God is involved. Learn to build the art of love for yourself and others and things will be much better for you. When you love for the good reasons, you are practicing the right dominion and authority over your life and other negativity.

# 10

## HAZAQ & CHAZAK

*Hazaq* and *Chazak* is a Hebrew word for *be strong* and *courageous* and a phrased used by God when he was having a conversation with Joshua before his installation as the next leader after Moses death. The Hebrew word 'hazaq' is taken from the scripture of Joshua 1:9, " I have I not commanded you? Be strong and courageous. Do not be afraid; do not be discouraged, for the LORD your God will be with you wherever you go. Now, if you can't Hazaq, then you will not take dominion, power or have authority over whatever is delaying or stopping you from going forward. God wants us to live in courage and not in fear. To be strong and courageous is the key to progress in life. Without strength, you can't have the courage to do daily activities, because strength and courage goes hand in hand. Courage is important, it's derived from strength.

Whilst examining this topic, I've discovered that courage is a characteristic for all believers and even none-believers. This is because when a believer has courage to do something and it works according to their consistency and faith, it then influences the unbelievers to believe and try too. Courage is a tool that can take you to the next level. For example, when you are climbing a long staircase, you tend to doubt if you can reach the top because of the pain and pressure you get on your knees. This often happens to those with physical impairments or other disabilities, despite this they are strong human beings. As this happens, you are thinking about what you need to get at the top and you are thinking about what's waiting for you at the top. But you are in agony and taking deep breaths, to help you hold on and continue. You are aware that, what you need at the top of the stairs is so important to you. So, in this kind of situation, you will need the courage to get you to the top or else, you could lose strength and easily give up. Now, when you give up, you lose that important thing waiting for you at the top, simply because you couldn't handle a temporary pain. But when you gain courage to deal with the pain and push forward to the next staircase, you will gain the prize waiting for you at the top. This is the power of courage; without it you can't accelerate, and you won't reach for your dreams. Courage helps you turn your dreams to reality. You need the audacity to have courage to do what is right, even if you're standing alone.

Courage makes you stand out from those who are forcing things that is not meant for them. But what will lead them to take away what's yours is their courage too. Now, this is a negative kind of dominion, but you need to prove them wrong by taking courage to do the right thing and get back what belongs to you. This is a positive dominion. To be able to win, you need courage, to be able to speak up, you need courage. In fact, you need courage to do everything and anything. Courage allows you breakthrough in such a way you would never have imagined. I recap writing about encouragement in my first book, but the Spirit of the Lord gave me more revelations and insights to elaborate and to go deeper on the subject, so we can understand the importance of Joshua 1:9 and why He emphasised on it. I just figured out that this is not a repeat but a reminder to me and you.

There was a man in the bible called Joseph who was a Levite from Cyprus. He was the one that the Apostles called Barnabas, which essentially means "Son of encouragement" (Acts 4:36). One thing about him I love is his heart and the powerful meaning of his name. He made use of the positive and powerful meaning of his name and took courage to sell his field. He took the courage to use the money he got from selling the field, for the purpose of the Kingdom of God.

Now, this is a positive way of taking dominion, power, and authority over your belongings and not to misuse it. It took him courage to do what is right. According to this, it's safe to say courage is an art we must develop. When you use encourage, it creates many beautiful things; I would also like to encourage you to carefully choose your names because what you are called is what you could eventually become. The meaning of your name has a massive role to play in your life, it practically has dominion over your life and can either shape or break you. When say you yes to becoming a Son of encouragement it means, you have accepted to practice positive dominion, power and authority by encouraging others to do better with their lives. When you have the spirit of encouragement, people would want to be around you, to get the opportunity of a lifetime, as they get the boost to be positive like you.

The ability to encourage others using the right words and being honest, impacts the person who's listening. Soon or later, you will watch the positive manifestation of your encouragements, in the lives of those you've allowed to grab the opportunity of a lifetime. This shows you're changing lives. You should be very proud of yourself, for being a Son of encouragement and not a destroyer. You've put the devil to shame by being an encourager of good and not evil. When someone is going through a hard time, whether a believer or not, encourage them to look at the positive sides of life, to see what they will gain, if they take courage to move forward and work hard for their happiness. Through this story, I've understood that it is crucial for believers to share their possessions for the glory of God because there's a reward behind it.

Now, I can see why God commands us to have courage and strength because it is the key to help us physically, so we can maintain our spiritual lives as well. It's for our own benefit. When we look at the first phrase of Joshua 1:9, the phrase "haven't I commanded you? is almost implying that God has already mentioned it to us. He believes Joshua was capable of leading, so all God was doing, at that moment, was to remind Joshua of it. This means that strength and courage is already in us, but we just need to activate it through the help of the Holy Spirit. God was also trying to make Joshua understand that its possible for him to lead, and that he doesn't need to be afraid, but have the courage to unleash the impossible and make it possible.

Through this scripture, God wants us to have a positive spirit and character in all circumstances, hence why he insists for us to be strong and courageous, using various words. God also knows and sees what will come in your life, that's why he says we shouldn't be afraid; this means we shouldn't give up. In other words, He is telling us to take dominion, power and authority over anything or anyone that will come our way to trigger fear in us. Know, that God has given us the spirit of power and not of fear, it's important for us to be bold in taking courage, so that positive dominion can be manifested in us. As the bible declares in 2 timothy 1:7 "For God hath not given us the spirit of fear, but of power and of love and of a sound mind". God always reminds us of our rights and what he has promised us as his children, for he knows we are only but human beings and can forget.

The word command also implies that we must do it, we have no choice. I've also noticed that in the bible, from Genesis to Revelation, God has not begged or asked anyone in terms of instructions but he sent and commanded people to follow His instructions, because He is the boss. God is so busy trying to fix people's lives, so He has no time to beg anyone but to send and command, so that his desire will be fulfilled. If His will is fulfilled in our lives, we will be happy but if His will is not fulfilled in our lives, we will not be happy either. That's why a lot of people's lives are in shambles and lacking peace because the will of God in their lives is still not yet achieved. In addition, God never forces anyone, he gives a choice as he commands or gives an instruction, it's up to you to follow it or not. When you don't obey his commands, it will always be your loss and not God's loss because he owns everything. When we disobey God's command, it shows a sudden disrespect and dishonour to Him. This is because we have decided to ignore God immediately, without thinking twice.

However, God never begs anyone for anything, all we need to know is that God is saying this for our own good because he also wants us to enjoy what he has created for us. But, to enjoy what he has created for us, it requires one condition, which is to hazaq in the Lord.

David, defeated Goliath and became a king, because he was strong and courageous. He never allowed himself to be afraid of Goliath because he knew the God of Israel was with him. Therefore, he was able to take dominion, power and authority over Goliath by finishing him and his evil plans completely. We cannot get victory if we are not strong and courageous to take dominion over our problems. How can you enter a battlefield without strength or courage? You will not come out alive because those weapons formed against you will prosper. So, if you don't want this to happen, you better take the courage to pray, so you can dominate. As a parent, you must also be strong and courageous to fight for your children and correct them when they are wrong. To do this, you need wisdom, patience, and love towards your children.

It is also crucial to have people around us, that can encourage and empower us to follow our dreams. Don't allow yourself to be around complainers, lazy, ignorant, discouraged people all the time because they will stop you from achieving your goals. The disciples were always around Jesus, that's why they impacted positively. Samuel was around Eli and he became David's destiny helper (1 Samuel 3). Elisha was around Elijah (2 Kings 2), Esther was around Mordecai (Esther 2:15), Ruth was around Naomi, that's why they all received the courage to become great people. Courage and strength will take you far in life and you will fulfil destiny, if God is by your side. Having the grace to encourage others positively as a child of God, shows you are doing the work of our Father in heaven, as he was also an encourager, whilst he preached the word of God. When you are courageous, it influences others to do the same, it's very contagious and almost like you are passing on a mantle or a disease.

Prayer Point: *Lord Jesus, grant me the spirit of courage and strength, so I can do better and empower others positively. In this new season of my life, make me a Son of encouragement for your glory, In Jesus name, Amen.*

# 11

# Unfolding Boldness, Toughness and Stubbornness

To have a dominion, power and authority, you've got to be very bold and tough because that makes you confident. On the other hand, there are also negative type of boldness and toughness in many of us. Don't be the kind of person who uses dominion to be tough on others in a bad way, otherwise people will think you are proud. Toughness is the quality of not being easily overpowered or made weaker because of a situation. Some people have been building this character by setting boundaries and to what they believe in. For example, some people may say to you", oh she has a reputation for toughness and resilience. This is an awesome way to practice your dominion, authority and power as a person.

It saddens me to see how many people use their boldness, toughness, and stubbornness in foolishness and think they are really doing well. Deception in all of this, is a kill joy because you lose the opportunity of a lifetime in front of those who are wise enough to see your potentials. But instead, they unfold the way you are using your boldness, toughness, and stubbornness. People of that nature, you can never deceive them because you will get caught. People who were stubborn, tough and bold for the wrong reasons, always end up in shame and disaster. If someone is stubborn, it means they are unmoving, obstinately maintained, and difficult to manage.

Now, this type of stubbornness is a negative dominion, power and authority, whether it's a child or an adult. For example, you have been warned not to go to a place because of danger, but you were stubborn and went. After getting to the place, for a little while someone blames you for another person's mistake of stealing in a shop, then the police were called, and you became a suspect. You end up getting arrested because of your stubbornness, despite being warned. Another example is when a friend has come to warn you about a certain friend who is stabbing you behind your back, but you were stubborn to listen, and the enemy has destroyed your name everywhere. In this case, you can't blame the person that gave you the news, they did a good job in informing to be careful and stay away that friend. Your stubbornness will lead you to trouble if you are not using it for the right reasons.

Another example is a child who doesn't listen to their parents and being very resistance whenever they are told off. These situations occur simply because of stubbornness and showing that you are tough and bold in a wrong environment. These situations fall under the negative use of dominion category, but it could have been avoided. Being stubborn, tough and bold in a bad way is also a form of witchcraft. Being a bully, a user, an abuser, a manipulator or a controller is not a synonym of toughness or boldness, it's not cute but it makes you look weak, foolish, loser and a beg. You can't go forward with a wrong way of stubbornness and toughness. These are all forms of a negative way of being stubborn, tough and bold in situations. However, the right way to be stubborn, tough and bold is when you are trying to do the right thing, but people are trying to stand against you.

For example, you are being forced to lie that you were never raped or molested, just to protect your family name, but you know that you were raped or molested. The pressure continues for you to keep your mouth shut and die in silence, but you are sticking to your point, which is the truth. Then, the family begins to call you stubborn, tough and bold, in a negative way. Now, this type of situation is the right way of being stubborn, tough and bold enough to speak up. It takes a lot for someone to be bold and tough in this situation because it is not easy to open to people, who you know that will never believe you. It also means that you were bold, tough and stubborn for the right reasons because you discovered how to unfold a raw truth hidden in you.

# 12
## The Gift of Listening

The Hebrew word *shema*, which means *listen* or *hear*. The first mention of the *shema* is founded in Deuteronomy. The bible teaches us that listening is more important than believing, as it brings grace, favour, and revival. The word *shema* also means obedience and to take actions. In other words, we need to obey God by hearing His voice as he speaks to us. The word of God says in Deuteronomy 6:4-9 "Hear, (or *Shema*) O Israel: The Lord our God, the Lord is one. You shall love the Lord your God with all your heart and with all your soul and with all your might and these words that I command you today shall be on your heart. You shall teach them diligently to your children and shall talk of them when you sit in your house, and when you walk by the way, and when you lie down, and when you rise. You shall bind them as a sign on your hand, and they shall be as frontlets between your eyes. You shall write them on the doorposts of your house and on your gates.

Therefore, you should listen, so that you can follow the exact instructions given to you, to dominate with power and authority. Listening exposes things that you didn't know that was said against you in a conversation. Listening will save you from danger. When you listen, it will expose evil clearly, as you pay attention to words entering your ears. We need to be careful on the kind of music we listen to and the kind of people we allow our ears to hear because they either dominate you in a positive or negative way. I hear many Christians say "Don't judge me", when they are caught listening to circular music and still minister to God's people. They only listen to gospel songs when in church or about to pray, sometimes they don't listen to any gospel songs at all. This is polluting your spirit and soul because its allowing demons instead of angels. This is a negative way of dominion, power and authority. It shows no difference between you as a Christian and the worldly. It's either what or who you are listening is representing God or the devil. Some of us may be saying right now, "Oh don't go there", but oh yes, we are going there because the kingdom of God is polluted by what enters our ears. This needs to stop. Remember, whatever you listen to has power, dominion, and authority over you, you will be eventually led by the songs you listen to and will begin to live by the words.

It is important that you master the art of listening because it will make you successful in life. The reason why I call listening a gift is because many people don't know how to listen. The bible says in Jeremiah 5:21, "Hear this, you foolish and senseless people, who have eyes but do not see, who have ears but do not hear". This implies We should understand that God is referring to our spiritual ears, the ability to have spiritual attentiveness. In other words, listening in the spirit. Most of us are not sensitive in the spirit and refuse to listen, that's why God called such people fools and senseless. Many people act like animals and not like human beings because they are fully aware that what they are listening to is not good for their soul, but they don't want to quit. The voice of the devil fights to dominate us, through listening to his evil instructions and discouragement. It's only foolish people who refuse to listen, when told to stop. These kinds of people will never be able to dominate positively, and they will become useless.

God reminds us again in Psalms 115:6, "They have ears but cannot hear, and noses but cannot smell." They have ears but they refuse to listen to good advice, it's almost saying that we are not using our 5 senses correctly. I can also say that listening has different colours to it, depending on what you hear and what you choose to absorb. I could also say it's an art because there are so many components hidden behind it, that you can work to put together and blend in if you focus on the details. Then, it will produce something colourful and touching. You might hear so many things, but it is for you to choose the right words to blend and build into an art. Remember, it's like choosing the right colour and knowing that it is something you can use to work on. When you listen well, you will produce something colourful, that will touch and bring hope in people's life. When you listen to good things and people, it's like putting in the right colours together that brings out a good blended and catchy image. It shows that you have chosen the right colours that befits you and can make you shine, brighten your day, week, month, and years. This will prove that you're taking the right dominion by listening to good advice that's leading you to pick the right colours. However, you must ensure that whatever befits you, what you listen to and the colour you choose, glorifies God. Remember, bad colours put together, is not good for the eye, neither for the ear because you will have to listen to the person explain the reasons for the bad colour combination. So, even when explained it's bad, why should you take time to listen to something that doesn't benefit you? All it will bring is negativity and darkness especially to a wounded soul.

The words you hear represents any existing colours in this world but it's how you use or take it in. So, for example, if you are in team yellow and others are in team blue; what you may hear team yellow say, may not be good for you. Therefore, you will take the good part of yellow and reject the rest of what's being said in team yellow. Then, focus on the good things said there, so you can use to create an art in team blue. If you listen, you will learn a lot, not necessarily practicing all you hear but gain knowledge that you never had before. It is important to listen and refrain from talking too much because you will be able to discover if someone is plotting against you or not, just by their words.

In James 1:19 God says, "Understand this, my dear brothers and sisters: You must all be quick to listen, slow to speak, and slow to get angry." You would notice that God uses the word 'all' to show who this word is for. It means that God is generalising and giving a lifetime opportunity for all, to listen and talk less because there's a blessing in listening. When you talk a lot, you can get yourself into trouble and lose the opportunity to listen. As a result, no one will bother to listen to you because they will know, you talk too much and refuse to listen to anyone else. This is lack of communication and it shows you have no power to control yourself. Abram was able to listen to God when he was instructed by God to sacrifice his only son Isaac. His obedience in listening to God saved and showed him that there's another sacrificial lamb for him. God did this so he can test Abram to see if he will remain faithful to him and he proved that by listening (Genesis 22). Most people talk a lot when they are preaching and what they are saying, makes sense but others just talk without thinking. In fact, it's very shameful not to listen, especially if it is for your own good and for the glory of God. God warns us to avoid anger because what you listen to can provoke anger, especially if you are spending your time listening to your enemies. I hear people say, you are what you eat, and I will also add, that you are who you listen to. Moreover, we need to be careful on what we intake as words, whilst listening to others because words echo back. Talking too much, will make you miss out on the most important things, especially whilst communicating with another. The bible says in Proverbs 10:19, "When words are many, transgression is not lacking, but whoever restrains his lips is prudent". This means that, if there's too many words coming out of your mouth, without control, you are at risk of doing mistakes and saying the wrong things. Therefore, the people listening may understand that you are feeding them with too many words that is not helping them. This also means; your words might cause others to sin but whoever controls her mouth is careful. Overall, we need to master the art of listening, so we can dominate, take authority and have power in the correct way, over every word projected into our ears. This is an opportunity of a lifetime for all to do and be successful in, but we need to be attentive and slow to speak.

Prayer point: *Lord Jesus, help me through the Holy Spirit to master my listening skills, that I will not be quick to talk but to listen more. Help me to control my tongue when I'm speaking so, I will not utter out sinful words. Purify my ears and mouth to avoid sin and to be prudent. Amen.*

# 13

## CROWDS: THE GOOD AND BAD

One of the ways of a crowd's mystery in our lives, is their toxic behaviours. Most of the time the crowd could be the source of your problems. You are only going to be as good as the people you surround yourself with, so be brave enough to let go of those who keep weighing you down.

Being in certain crowds can lead to distractions, noisy, chaotic situations. I view this type of crowd as peer pressure because some of them are very influential in a negative. They will use others to unite, just to fight you, as they did to Jesus. Moreover, if you look straight in their circle, they have serious issues between them. They hate on each other and will gather only when they are ready to attack you. Personally, I've had a very bad experience with the crowd, they made me do things I never thought I would do in life. This happened not once or twice but severally because I was naïve and lonely, so I followed the crowd to fit in when I was younger. In addition, my marriage has always been attacked by the crowd, but I've never had to fight so hard against my husband. It has always been the outsiders that troubled us. It was not due to us letting them in but because the crowd forced themselves on us through my maternal family member. This occurred through the permission of our families and people we knew in the community and not through our own consents. The crowd were jealous of how peaceful and blessed we are as a couple and individually. So, the crowd gathered to fight and cause chaotic scenes in our lives, trying to make us offenders instead of the victims that we were. Bad crowds come with bad motives but know how to deal with them once you know them. This is a bad way of dominance, power, and authority over people. Classify and put them into the groups they belong or fall into. Some crowds come with hunger, with a heart of vengeance, In the bible it says that, after the crowd was fed, they were satisfied but there were still leftovers of the loaves and fishes. At a certain point, the same crowd who praised Jesus, were the same who influenced and insisted to Pilate that Jesus should be crucified. The disciples picked up 12 basketfuls of broken pieces that were leftovers. We can use this as a metaphor to elaborate that people can be basketfuls with food, money and all the good things in this world, and still be broken pieces. On top of that, they still become leftovers by people who are tired of them. In life, you can eat as much as you want but at some point, you will get tired and leave what's left. The crowds had just enough but it was still not enough to make them appreciate Jesus.

On the other hand, crowds can also be a blessing to us because they help us discover who we really are in the public eye. You can also meet lovely people whilst with crowds, but you must be very selective. Some crowds gathered to destroy Jesus; others gathered against those who believed in Jesus, but some crowds still believed in Jesus. For example, a crowd of people marching for a good cause in the society, can be a good way of socialising and meeting other citizens. You never know who your destiny helper could be, so always have an approachable and an observational attitude.

Regarding the number of basketfuls and the disciples, I see a numerical connection. Therefore, I've analysed that 12+12=24 or in other words, Basketful +disciples equal returned. So instead of losing, they gained double of their blessing, then it increased in number. Numbers in the bible has significant meanings and its always powerful and life changing. This addition is another revelation of its own and we'll discover it, right here.

Let's grab a lifetime opportunity to know the mysteries of number 12 and 24 below: Firstly, number 12 is also associated to the main topic of this book which is power and authority. I'm beginning to understand that God wants us to capture something that would benefit us all. The meaning of 12, is measured as a perfect number. It denotes God's power and authority and assists as a perfect governmental foundation. It can also represent completeness or the nation of Israel in full.

For example, Jacob (Israel) who was the son of Isaac, conceived twelve sons and each of which represented a tribe begun by a prince, for 12 princes total. Ishmael, who was born to Abraham through Hagar, also had twelve princes.

Number twelve also shows when Christ called and chose twelve men to witness to his works and to spread the gospel to the whole world. It happened later, that Jesus was raised from the dead, He informed the eleven disciples (Judas had killed himself) that God gave him all power and authority over the earth and heaven. This is called God's divine authority, which is found in Matthew 28:18. I've noticed that number twelve represents the anointed ones for a special duty just as Solomon selected twelve officers over Israel. Number twelve is for the chosen and identified for a mission. Jesus knew who was able to go with him to the mission God gave him, so he gave them an opportunity of a lifetime. God saw their willing hearts towards Him and trusted them to carry on with spreading the good news of the Gospel. The number 24 is connected to the priesthood, as it's a multiple of 12, it takes on some of the 12s meaning, which is God's power and authority, as mentioned above. 24 is also connected to the worship of God, especially at the temple, for our body is the temple of God. I will encourage all of us to give your body a lifetime opportunity to worship God. It also represents people who are responsible for the music in temple services, those who served as priests, and the Levites who helped the priests, into 24 courses (1 Chronicles 23 - 24). In Psalm 72 of David's prayer, there are 24 things that Jesus Christ, as High Priest after the order of Melchizedek, will do when He sits upon His throne and rules as King and Priest during that time; the list includes:

1.  He will righteously judge the people

2.  He will judge, with justice, the poor and needy

3.  Peace will be brought by the mountains

4.   Small hills shall also experience peace

5.   He shall judge the poor

6.   He shall save the children of the needy

7.   Those who oppress will be crushed

8.   He shall rule like rain upon grass

9.   He shall rule like the water that showers the globe

10.  He will cause the righteous to flourish

11.  He will bring the righteous an abundance of peace

12.  He shall rule from sea to sea

13.  He shall rule from the river unto the ends of the earth.

14.  When he hears the needy cry out, he will deliver him

15.  The poor and those who have no help will also be delivered

16.  Those who are needy and weak will receive compassion

17.  The lives of those in need will be saved

18.  The needy who are oppressed, and experience violence will be redeemed

19.  The blood of those in need will be precious in His sight

20.  He will cause an abundance of grain on the earth

21.  He will bring an abundance of fruit

22.  He will make those of the city flourish like grass

23.  He will make His name to be continued

24.  He will bless all men

This is considered as a positive dominance because it's a lifetime opportunity for all, but you must work to be entitled to it. It could also signify that the disciples were twelve broken pieces before, but Jesus came to satisfy them and those around them (the crowd). So, they also benefited from what the crowds received because they picked up the leftovers. The crowd were also broken pieces but when they met Jesus, they left satisfied as they fed them (Luke 9:17). At times, don't be too harsh on the crowd but be vigilant and resilient because some of them can be good to you by protecting and speaking for you. Crowds can be the ones helping you to get to the next level, they are like our stairs. So, at times, don't be too harsh on the crowd but be vigilant and resilient because some of them can be good to you by protecting and speaking for you.

In Luke 9:18- it mentions about who do the crowd say I am? Jesus asked the disciples: so, what would people, the crowd, the enemies say about you. Jesus prayed privately, even when his disciples was with him. Crowds are followers, they are like flies, as they form a crowd when they perceive something, whether good or bad. It is important to be a follower of good things and follow Jesus because He is the way truth and the life. I realise that Herod Tetrarch was (Luke 9:1) also part of the crowd, as he too followed what the crowd said who Jesus was. The crowd will follow you, when you have Jesus, just like the crowd learned about it and followed him. They will learn that you did something, but let that something be about Jesus and, nothing else. No to gossips, no fights, trouble but good things only. Whilst there's a crowd, take all the opportunity to welcome and speak to others about the kingdom of God and heal those who needs it. When you have power and authority people will obey you, due to the influence you have on them. This is also called dominion but ensure you have the authority and power from God and not from the devil.

This is a way to treat the crowd, with care and peace. In order to do this, you must be prepared, filled with the Holy Spirit, power, authority and dominion. Don't just send the crowd away, without having anything reasonable to say to them. The disciples mentioned that the crowds should be sent to safe places with a message of encouragement, find them food, lodges because you are in a remote place. In the things of God, sometimes be immediate, don't wait for the next crowd or next person to reply or do what you can do. During a crowd, allow your voice to be heard too. When you can speak, object your voice, you are already exercising some level of dominance and authority. It is also important to be around those who have power, authority and dominance and use it the right way. It can also be an act of fellowship. Just like the disciples, they were with Jesus who was using his power, authority and dominance positively. In Luke 9:16 I've notice that only the disciples could distribute the loaves and bread and no one else. So, you must be instructed, ordained, dominant to distribute the communion. Not everything is to be said. In order to take dominion, you need to deny yourself and take up your cross daily to follow Jesus, not sometimes but to follow Jesus (Verse 23).

In Luke 12: 35, we can say that in order to dominate, you need to be watchful and stay awake because the consequences of not being watchful can be costly. You can be stripped off your power, authority and the ability to dominate if you are asleep. Dominance is not for the sleepy neither for the weak. A person who is asleep can never dominate because whilst sleeping your body is no longer functioning in the same manner as to when awake. You will miss out on a lot, that's why lazy people sleep a lot and rely on others. Don't even think of relying on people to do your assignment, otherwise they will take dominion over what's yours and your will lose. But instead, rely on Jesus Christ to lead you, so you can take dominion over what has your name on it. You will have to dominate in the right way and be intentional no matter what it involves. We also must ensure that whatever we have dominion on, is giving glory to God. In that manner, we can say that we have dominated positively, by not destroying others but in building others. This is true and genuine dominance.

In Luke 9:26 God says if you are ashamed of God and His words, you'll not be able to have dominion affectively and He will deny you. This will lead to you being ashamed of yourself as well because it's only by the word of God that Christians can be effective if dominion must be practiced positively in the world. Without the power, authority of God, you cannot have dominion the way God intended. Sharing the word of God will bring you dominance, power and authority because people will listen to you. A Christian who feels uncomfortable, scared to serve God or speak about Jesus Christ Infront of their peers has serious issues because you can't please God this way. Moreover, a shy person can't affectively take dominion if they don't overcome their shyness. Timidity will always lose great opportunities, instead of dominating the shyness, kicking it out and to go ahead of it. People who have stage frights struggle to perform because of fear and anxiety.

Jesus was trying to also teach us the practice of discretion when he warned the disciples not tell anyone about it. So, I guess it was a way to teach us on seasons and waiting on God's time before you can dominate.

Holiness: Living a life of holiness is not the act of wearing vail over your head and remaining silent. But living a holy life is the act of pleasing God and respecting yourself. Imagine, if you were asked to marry a prostitute or a homosexual person as a Christian, you would refuse because they are committing acts of impurity. As a normal person, some may agree to be in a relationship with these kinds of people, but a Christian shouldn't be okay with it, unless it's the will of God.

The reason I say this is because I watched a United Kingdom reality show about relationships, a woman was not comfortable with dating a gay person but I'm not too sure if she was a believer of Christ or not. But she made her point clear and the man also made it clear that he will remain gay and nothing can change that, not even a female. So, as a Christian is very important to live a life sold to God, so that even the person you marry will see and agree to that. When you live a holy life, it causes people to respect, honour and consider you. People won't even dare to disrespect you because they see how you respect and carry yourself. Now, this is called authentic dominance because you are doing things right and people will have no choice than to be impacted. This implies that your positive way of living has allowed you to take dominion. According to the Christian bible, people who practice homosexuality are committing an abomination, this is a negative way of dominance, as it doesn't please God. In Leviticus 20:13 it says, "If a man has sexual relations with a man as one does with a woman, both of them have done what is detestable. They are to be put to death; their blood will be on their own heads.

Now, God will not only punish the man but also the woman who practices this because they are dominating others negatively through a sinful lifestyle. I am not saying this to condemn such people but to speak the truth that is facts from the bible that all Christians should be aware of, as God does not rejoice in the death of a sinner but He wants the sinner to repent and they will be saved. Jesus loves everyone, but He detests the sin we commit, as it destroys our soul and makes us lose the power, he's given to us to dominate over everything.

As it's declared in Genesis 1:26-28 Then God said, "Let us make man in our image, after our likeness. And let them have dominion over the fish of the sea and over the birds of the heavens and over the livestock and over all the earth and over every creeping thing that creeps on the earth."

So, God created man in his own image. If you still don't know, I need you to understand that it's a great privilege and honour to be given this opportunity. I mean, this is an opportunity of a lifetime for all, we can just believe in Jesus. God created humans and gives them the care they need. By God giving humans dominion over the land and animals, He's giving humanity the right to govern and have power over all other living beings.

You must know that taking dominion is a big responsibility of its own and that means, you don't play jokes with it, as it involves not only you, but other hearts too. Taking dominion, is the idea of taking charge, serving, building, motivating, speaking, thinking out loud and being bold within and in the outward. This also means, you must take charge, dominion over your problems, setbacks, trials, persecutions and tribulation. No one else will do it for you, unless you do it yourself. Dominion is like taking personal convictions, if you are not convicted, you will never be able to dominate. To take dominion means you know who you are, your identity and what you stand for and what you represent. Whatever you choose to dominate is who you are, so choose wisely the things you choose to dominate. To dominate also means influence because people will listen to your instructions and principles when you carry dominion.

The Christian bible also says in Leviticus 18:22 "Do not have sexual relations with a man as one does with a woman; that is detestable." So, a person who really fears God, lives a holy life and is in their senses, why would they be very comfortable in such a union? You can't dominate positively if you get yourself in such union because it's sinful and can cause death. Each time we sin, we die spiritually but if we call on the blood of Jesus to dominate in us and cleanse us, we become pure and will be resurrected.

However, God says in Romans 6:14, "For sin will have no dominion over you, since you are not under law but under grace". In addition, we can't be equally yoked with people who don't have the same conviction as us, not to run away from them but not to do what they do. As the bible declares in 2 Corinthians 6:14 "Don't team up with those who are unbelievers. How can righteousness be a partner with wickedness? How can light live with darkness? I mentioned a similar example as the above scripture about relationships. You see, I love the fact that the New Living Translation version of this scripture uses the word 'team up' to clearly describe what God wants us to understand.

The person you get involved with can determine your destiny and purpose It will determine whether you will have the capacity to dominate what is coming ahead of you or not. Many people have no ability to take dominion of their destiny, purpose or anything crucial in their lives because you've teamed up with the wrong people. This is caused by lack of knowledge and understanding. Once you sort these two out, in terms of dominion, you are halfway to be *good to go* in different areas of life.

When you team up with the wrong crowd, you become stuck and delayed. You can only dominate effectively with the right people. In my past life, I teamed up with the wrong people and wrong relationships that nearly cost my life but thank God for His saving grace upon my life. I can now say that, I've now taken dominion over my destiny and purpose because I'm living in it. So, I ask "Are you living in your destiny and purpose in order to take the right dominion?"

God didn't create Adam and Adam or Eve and Eve, but he created Adam and Eve for a positive purpose. This implies that, gay and lesbianism is not to be practiced. Therefore, we should do what God requires of us in the bible and not your own will. When you allow the will of God to prevail, it means you will indeed dominate and have great influence on people. The dominion God gave us was not to harm people but to serve God's people with it. But When we use it wrongly, trouble comes.

# 14
## GOVERNMENTS

God didn't not give us dominion as children of God to manipulate or to look down on others neither to take advantage of people. If you are in a higher position than others, treat them right. this implies to serve the people, taking the right measure of dominion over them. It also means never overdose it because you will come out of the principles of dominion as a leader. Your heart needs to first take dominion over any hatred, envy, greediness, or anything negative living in you, that's against the nation and God. Revenge shouldn't be the reason why you misuse dominion. The right way to take dominion, as you are leading your country is through wisdom, knowledge, understanding and having the fruits of the Holy Spirit. All this, God gives freely, only ask and it will be yours, as it declares in Matthew 7:7 "Ask and it will be given to you; seek and you will find; knock and the door will be opened to you". How can you take dominion if there's no equality in you? that means you will not lead affectively.

The power and authority God has given to you is also to transmit it to your workers, so they can take over when you are not present. You have the dominion to change what's not right in the country, but you have no right to change the good in the country into a bad thing because that will be going against human rights and what the nation wants. Dominion also means to conquer and to be a winner by making other winners. Being able to take dominion also shows that you are a warrior, born to win and not to lose because a warrior needs to also have the character of dominion. God says, "No, in all these things we are more than conquerors through him who loved us" (Romans 8:37).

This means in everything, we must conquer and take dominion whenever we can, which refers us back to Genesis 1:26-28, where God officially gives us the dominion over everything. Therefore, I encourage you to never be afraid, never give up and go and dominate your enemies who are trying to pull you down from being great and doing what is right for your country. Remember, as a child of God, president, minister, journalist, or whatever role you are called to serve the people in, you have the power, dominion and authority over them and your enemies too.

Things such as education, should be improved and not stopped or attacked by the governments, due to the benefits of their own stomachs. King Solomon is a perfect example of this as he was a king and God gave him the power, riches, authority and dominion. Later, God then granted him wisdom as he requested, in order to lead the people God gave him. To have dominion as a leader, also signifies kingship but it doesn't mean you should boss people about as if they have no value, no voice or in a low background. You will probably be very shocked to hear that, the ability to take dominion is also the act of equality, so treating everyone equal.

Honestly speaking, nobody wants to be dominated by someone who doesn't treat them equally; especially if you are in your right senses. But most of the time if your brain is regulating well, you won't allow anyone who discriminates, dominate you because equality will not be in their dictionary. Even, people who are mad mentally can sense at times when someone is trying to hurt them physically, bully or treating them unequally because they will say certain things that has a meaning and will have you think twice. The reason being is because madness can put you in a state where you control things and actions around you, but in a foolish state, things and events can be destroyed. Just like drinkers, when they are drunk, some of them can still drive and know what's happening. Some of them can still manage to pick up the bottle of wine, so it's possible for an individual whose brain is regulating normally to control themselves and do the right thing.

Another example is when I watched a police documentary on channel 5, on 6th January 2022, where a police officer in UK arrested a man who was drinking alcohol and spat on the police officer. He still had the power to hold his can of alcohol and communicating but being violate at the same time. The offender was charged to prison for 52 weeks. This is to show you that people who don't do the right things, can also control themselves and know exactly what they are doing. My point is, they should be able to control themselves and know when to stop behaving negatively. Meaning that all governmental officials must have self-control and stop practicing negative dominion, power and authority over citizens. If a drunken or a mad person can behave well, communicate, and have self -control at some point; presidents, ministers and leaders of the country should do the same. A positive conducted is expected of all government officials as they role models to many citizens of the country.

It's also the same as a couple, as the head of the home is the husband, no wife would submit to a man who can't dominate right or treat them with equality. There must be a balance, if I must submit, you need to treat me right. If you want the people to submit to you as the president, you must treat them equally and right. As someone working in the government, don't be like King Saul who was rebuked by Samuel and rejected by God. His disobedience caused him to lose his kingship, the crown. So, instead of him being promoted, he was rejected by God, as the country's leader. Saul's failure to follow God's instructions concerning the "prohibition" is the most serious disobedience and it resulted In Samuel's corroding rebuke: "Because you have rejected the word of the LORD, he has also rejected you from being king" (1 Samuel 15:23). If you can't dominate right, someone else who can, will take over by force. Just like David took over the throne after king Saul's fall. In some countries, dogs are treated equally then humans, how much more with human beings, the people God has entrusted you with? making sure you dominate and lead right as the country's leader is essential.

Prayer: *Lord help me to dominate discrimination, disobedience, inequality in my leadership as a president or a member of the government. May I not take your people for granted; may I not take advantage of their weaknesses. May I not be corrupted by anyone to steal what belongs to your people. As I lead the country you've entrusted me with, Lord, may the fruit of the Holy Spirit be my character, help me to dominate positively, in Jesus's name, Amen.*

# 15

## HYPOCRISY VS PRETENDING

I've personally discovered that there's different ways of pretending but I've selected two of which that caught my eyes, it will be explained below in this book. There's hypocrisy type of pretending and amusement type of pretending, such as a role play. By the way, this is not a free will or a giveaway to grab a lifetime opportunity in becoming a hypocrite toward others. It's not nice, don't be a hypocrite in a sense of destroying others. However, informing someone about a negative plan you heard against them, is not being a hypocrite but it's called, "Saving a life". It's only those who don't want the person to know about their evil plan towards their victim, will feel offended and call you a hypocrite. They are mad because you've exposed them and saved another's life from remaining an ignorant.

However, one thing that I've also observed, which is certain; everyone has some level of hypocrisy which I also consider as a pretending act. Whether you agree with me or not, I know that we all have a drop of hypocrisy behaviour in us, hidden somewhere. This drop of hypocrisy occurs when you are trying to avoid someone or something, so you tend to either pretend or distance yourself around certain people. It could also be an act of pretending when you're trying to be someone else or do something that's not corresponding to your personality.

In addition, others could just be acting for the time being, either to be satisfied or to frustrate others. But you see the problem with this whole pretending issue is, you can't keep up with it for too long. There's nothing wrong with pretending sometimes but it must be controlled or else it could lead to hypocrisy. When you pretend with a hatred, malice and a jealous heart it leads to hypocrisy. However, the 'joke' kind of pretending is not to be taken too personal because it's just a joke or for amusements. Children tend to use this phrase a lot, "I'm just pretending mama". Sometimes adults do this too. There were times I would play games with my child and will say, "Mama let's play the pretending game." And we would play games such as singing, dancing, rebuking, or correcting each other and we would laugh whilst doing it. For my child, this simply meant that we should play a game that's not taken too seriously.

Sometimes, if care is not taken, it could go wrong, others will get angry and take it too personal when it was meant to be a joke. Now, this is where the topic of dominion comes in because you can't dominate if you don't quit hypocrisy or continue to take things too personal (Luke 12:54). Learn to laugh, be strategic, wise, understanding when it comes to pretending but not hypocrisy. Especially if you are fully aware of the person laughing with you but killing you behind your back. You will need to dominate them by changing your way of living around their company progressively, then finally quit your relationship with them in a calm manner. This particular action of pretending doesn't mean that you had planned to hurt the enemy but to defend yourself before they hurt you. You would wisely do it by just collecting information of their evil acts towards you and then back off immediately, without hurting them. The information you collect, is not for you to use it against them but to keep for future references, so in urgency or danger.

When you do this, it means that you have been pretending from the minute you discovered the hidden agenda they had against you. In this kind of situation, you would become more reserved around the person and slowly detach yourself from them. This Is for your own safety and precautions. Reacting in this manner doesn't make you a hypocrite, but it makes you a wise person and shows that you were very precautious. This proves that you wouldn't want to be a hypocrite but to pretend for observation or investigation purposes, then execute after collecting vital information. As a Christian, to protect your peace, mind, and soul, you need to dominate the devil by cancelling his plots against you through prayer by pretending as if you don't know of his plans, but not for too long. This will show the power and authority you have as a child of God before people.

There's also another category of people who practice the hypocrisy type of pretending and that's normally the wrong way of taking dominion. For example, there was a woman who was a colleague of mine in ministry and a friend to my husband. I planned a woman programme with other ladies, and she was also included. She sent me her pictures for the flyer, but after telling me of her husband's input concerning the programme, that he won't be involved. When this woman saw that a friend of mine, who is also a prophetess, was going to be there, she now called telling me that she can't be on the same flyer as my friend due to her bad past.

She began speaking about my friend, looking down and literally just writing her off but I realised that she was gossiping about my friend. So, I stopped her and told her to give my friend a chance, as she's a human too and is seeking for love, acceptance due to rejection of the community and her family. I had to make it clear to her that people's past does not determine their future, she's trying to serve her God, so let's allow her to do that. Although, she was hesitating at my words, at the end she agreed with me and we finished the conversation there. A few days later, I discovered from my friend that the woman paid a surprise visit to her house, they ate, laughed, and had a great time. I was shocked to hear this because the woman initially told me that because she's my friend, we would go and see her together, but she went behind my back and thought I wouldn't find out. I don't know what her plan was then or now, but I was not happy with her behaviour at all, she took dominion over me and my friend in a wrong way. That behaviour proved to me that, she is a jealous, envy and a proud hypocrite, as she was killing someone mentally and destroying her reputation but still went to eat her food. This is another high level of evilness.

In addition, she ordered more chicken from the same woman she gossiped about and refused to be in the same flyer as her. She fed her husband with the same chicken she ordered from my friend and doesn't even feel guilty for doing that. When I found out about this, I was sick for one week. I couldn't sleep, I had nightmares concerning her, and I couldn't call her again. So, what I decided to do is to distance myself from her slowly, calmly because I realise that she is controlling, manipulating, monitoring people's lives and a very dangerous person.

I had to do this, because I am not a hypocrite but pretended for some time when I discovered her true colours. I did this to protect myself from such person as they were trying to even invade in my privacy. The type of hypocritical behaviour she performed was a hatred one and not the one where, you are being a hypocrite to protect yourself, like I previously explained in this book. So, I and my husband, concluded that, if she can do this to my friend, that means she can certainly do it to us too. I got frustrated even more when she acts like nothing is happening. She thinks I have no idea about what she did behind my back and still commenting lovely comments on the same woman she gossiped and ordered chickens from. She would try to comment negatively about my outfits but would go crazy if I said anything about her daughter's way of dressing in church. Another thing she done, was to tell me what my haters called her to say about me but refused to tell me the name of the lady. So, I wondered why she would tell me nonsense, without mentioning the name. I was beginning to lose my patient with her each time we met. Moreover, I hated the way she would give me advice to do with ministry and my personal things Infront of her daughter. I approached her about it and showing that I was not happy with what she did, but she was offended.

I even asked her if we can discuss further in another room, but she was offended too and refused by trying to cover up that the conversation was over. She repeated the behaviour for the second time, even in the car and I kept on holding my tongue because I didn't want to be rude to her. I began to analyse that she really had a negative power, authority, dominion, and control over me. I thought I was doing the right thing to remain respectful, but I didn't know that I was hurting myself by allowing her to use me. I truly thought I could find a mother in her and tell her anything, but I was wrong in the end.

During this relationship, at some point I felt I was forcing myself and being forced at the same time. It was like doing everything to please her and not myself. This was not fair at all, as she realised from my behaviour, but she refused to change or communicate. Her character was affecting me even at home with my husband, that we would argue concerning her. My husband was telling me to leave her, but I just wanted to give her another chance, a I believed she will change but I was totally wrong. I smelt betrayal in her behaviour, and I had to run for my life before it was too late. I don't know if she treated me this way because I am younger than her or was more experienced then me in ministry, and thought I was stupid, blind or clueless and that I would not discover who she truly is, but God made me dominate her malice ways. This situation reminds me of the story Judas Iscariot, who betrayed Jesus Christ to his enemies. Judas Iscariot was communicating with Jesus's enemies behind his back, and he thought Jesus wouldn't know about his evil plan.

This act of negative dominion was exactly what this woman pastor did to me. As soon as I discerned it and said enough is enough, I had to stand my ground because her jealousy, fake love, fake advise was exposed by God. As the word of God says, "And Judas, who betrayed Him, also knew the place; for Jesus often met there with His disciples (John 18:2). Your enemies will know the place you go to and cooperate with your friends just to harm you, but when you discover and try to ask them, they will deny or feel offended.

God also says in John 18:5, "They answered Him, "Jesus of Nazareth." Jesus said to them, "I am He." And Judas, who betrayed Him, also stood with them. This proves that those who are ready to kill you with your enemies are always standing by you, they are never far.

So, I ask, would you like to be close or to allow such person in this case, take dominion over you? I don't think so.

I share this to show us how people are dominating others in the wrong way. In some way, she has impacted my life negatively for the little time I knew her. But thank God for discernment and prayer life he has given to me, so I can collect vital information, then distance myself. People like this have so much pride and will never accept their wrong but I would recommend deliverance process for a change of character in them. It's a sad reality, seeing both becoming friends to be attacking and throwing tantrums against me on social media. Nevertheless, I laugh with pity for them because if only my friend knew what she did and say against her, they would not be talking and deceiving themselves. But for the sake of peace, I choose to keep quiet and pray that God reveals the truth to my friend. Months after this incident, we decided to visit my friend, as she was looking forward to seeing us for the first time, so we went. We had to inform her of what the lady pastor has been doing and saying concerning her, so she doesn't stay ignorant. She was very happy that we informed her, and she told us that, she sensed something very weird about her, but she couldn't place her finger on it. She continued thanking us for letting her know about evil thoughts this lady pastor had against her, then we went home.

Later that week, my friend refused to respond to my messages or to pick up my calls. I wished her son a happy birthday, she read it but never responded, so I stopped communicating with her. I have no clue what I did wrong. I realised she commented lovely things to the lady pastor, after all we informed her. I was shocked, in how foolish and inconsiderate some people can be, after being warned about your enemy. Instead, she stopped talking to us that was genuinely trying to save her life. On that day, I learnt to just let some people stay in their misery and ignorance, as they don't deserve my help or from saving their life against their enemies. What we did for this woman, no one in our community would have the energy to do that, we were trying to be kind, to listen and stick up for her, when her enemies were killing her from a distance. I just leave her case in the hands of God, may the Lord have mercy on both, I'm out of it.

Ever since, I took this decision, I feel so light and free within me, knowing that I have no hate for them, concerning this situation and things are working for my good because I've learnt to take the right dominion over my enemies.

There are some individuals who have the right type of the dominion, which is evident. An example of this is my husband, he can capture someone or people's mind and attention when he is talking, through advice or rebuking. I've seen it a lot where others will refuse to listen to someone else saying the same thing as him but would rather listen to my husband. In this kind of situation, others are attention seekers and force people to listen to them. This is a wrong way of dominance, power, and authority.

Another situation I've seen with my husband is when a man asked him to preach and speak about fornication, he agreed, and people listened to him. But when the pastor was asked to do the same thing, the man declared that he couldn't say it because the congregation will not listen to him. I find this quite funny because they both had the duty of saying the same thing, but one couldn't deliver it. This shows that there's a way of delivering things. I've understood that the pastor, didn't have dominion over fornication because he still practiced it. You can't rebuke or speak against something easily that has dominated you, it will not come out and the people you address it to will never listen to you because they will know deeply that you are one of them.

This means you have not mastered that sin; it is still dominating you. You can receive the same word as someone else but the way to deliver it, is always different. The one who can deliver the message without insulting or hurting but causing people to understand them, has practiced the right dominion. Moreover, you would notice that people who practice the right dominion, have a positive impact on others because multitude of lives are transformed through their voice and good actions. I see this as a gift and can also be the nature of the person. This type of dominion goes hand in hand with wisdom, power and authority. To those who take dominion the right way, I want you to know that you are performing miracles, without knowing.

Prayer point: *Father in heaven, deliver me from the spirit of hypocrisy, hate, envy and jealousy. Give me the strength to take dominion over manipulating and controlling spirit living in me, that's destroying other people's lives, deliver me Lord. , Grant me discernment, so I can know who is for me and who is not for me In Jesus name, Amen.*

# 16

## CHURCH LEADERS

To take the right dominion, a true leader must not gossip or talk negatively about their church members to others. Again, I repeat, as leaders we need to be eagles that can see from afar and sense when something is not right. Your church members are under your umbrella, so it's important you have the right dominion over them, that will benefit and not harm them. I've experienced a woman saying all sorts of malice against her church members. I was quite disturbed because she portraits herself in a very holy image and that she doesn't mind people's business, but she minds people's business. The pastor will utter things like, "Oh don't mind her, she's pretending to live a luxury life... she's a witch... she's a show-off... she lives on benefits... The car she has is an old model... She's even a prostitute and changes men all the time". She even warned me from her church members that I shouldn't allow them to be close to me. But she was the same person telling me to open to them but being overprotective, as well as diminishing them in my presence.

For the fact that she is the type who never likes corrections and will find offense in anything she doesn't agree with, I couldn't even warn her about how she leads her church members. I know some people may say, who am I to tell her how to lead her church members, but I have the duty to correct her in love, however, it was impossible to do so in her case. The woman pastor kept on doing this and it was draining me. I began to avoid her presence or even to call her on the phone, when she referred to another pastor as a mad woman, after inviting and praising her before the congregation. I realised that the relationship was becoming toxic and leaving me sad most of the time.

So, I shared it with my husband, and he suggested that I step back and focus on other things and I did just that. But the woman pastor began to feel offended that I don't call her no more and I've abandoned her. God has taught me on how to respond to certain people, especially if I know their reactions during a correction. I replied, I was busy on other things, just for peace to reign, I hate chaos, trouble around me but people love bringing trouble to me and if I react, I become the bad one, so I always ask God to remove those kinds of people around me. We need to learn to stop that religious behaviour of only watching other people's mistakes and forgetting your own. We need to lead by examples and dominate correctly and to stop chaos in the church. God will ask us to give an account of the souls of the church members he entrusted us with. Supporting your church members and being there for them is very crucial.

I was in a situation that almost made me act in a very foolish manner but thank God for calmness and the spirit of discernment. A sister I worked with in ministry where she invited me into her programme. She joined my woman ministry WhatsApp group, but hardly participated and we had the same issues with other ladies in there. Therefore, my team were complaining about that behaviour, then I felt as a leader, I had to act and reach out to each member. So, I reached out to two ladies, I explained to them calmly and considering their occupations and they were very understanding. So, they apologised and reassured me that they will make amends and the communication went well and ensured them that they shouldn't feel pressured but to at least value the team leader's efforts. Another lady I reached out to with a prayer before telling her about the same issue, but she completely misunderstood me, despite apologising after I finished speaking. Towards the end of the conversation, she started shouting on top of her voice, refusing to let me explain the use of my context as I mentioned to her that some people are human but don't act like they are humans due to their negative behaviour and neglect to other people. I tried my best to end the conversation in good terms with her and told her that we are not quarrelling, it's all love and that she shouldn't take it too personal.

Despite my efforts, the next morning I saw a 4 paraph message from her complaining and even insulting me, with so many accusations. I was gobsmacked, shocked and tired, so I replied to her with a simple, "Hey, thank you for the message, God bless you." She read my message and never replied yet she's someone that serves in a church too. I discerned in my spirit that it was a spiritual attack. I've never disregarded her personal issues when she reached out to me and always showed concerned and encouraged her to take things easy.

In my heart, I just said if only she knew that I always pray and mean well for her, she wouldn't say those negativities against me. I began to think if an evil spirit possessed her, which led her to that extend. I was in so much pain, knowing that she took things so far. She probably thought I would return the same insults back at her but the fact that I am not the type, I had to just let it go. I even messaged her a few days later to see how she's doing and require about a product she sent me. However, she was replying like someone that doesn't want to talk and I realised that she blocked me from seeing her WhatsApp statuses but liked my face book post, so I just moved on with my life. Throughout this whole time, I was praying for her and I kept on doing it, so God gave me peace concerning her. In all these cases, I had to practice pastoral deontology when it comes to church leadership.

Another reality, I experienced, was when I was consulted by a sister who is younger than me. She and her friends were having a dispute with another sister. The sister reached out to me, asking if I can speak to the sister who blocked her and other sisters on Instagram but was still following one of their fiancé's. I advised and agreed to speak with the sister causing the chaos. When I tried to speak to the sister in question, she was very rude towards me. I felt so humiliated and said to myself, that I will not accept to help resolve another sister's dispute because it was a disrespect to my person. A few months later, I saw all the sisters who were arguing before, now become friends. I was shocked and just laughed, I understood that it was the devil's hand work to tempt me but thank God I just stepped back. I discovered that the Zimbabwean sister blocked me everywhere on all social media platforms. Then, a few months later I found that she unblocked me again, but never reached out to apologise. She forgot how I helped and supported her ministry works and the good relationship we had. I stayed on the phone quiet, listening to her bragging about how she has people who mentors her but still can't communicate or see her wrongs. You can't lead people with this kind of character. That's why Proverbs 12:15 says, "The way of fools seems right to them, but the wise listen to advice". After trying to speak with her to reach out to the ladies, she wronged and apologise but she refused, I felt like I was wasting my time.

I find it difficult to understand people that cause chaos and mix up between others, then pretend to be victims. These are the kind of people to avoid in life. They will be quick to provoke but slow to fix the problem at hand; they will blame others and make themselves look good. Now, when I look at all of them, I just laugh and give glory to God for saving me from whatever plot they had. After this situation, I prayed for the sister who caused the problem and along with the sisters who sought for my help in between. I tried to help but it was rejected and misunderstood by the prideful sister. Out of my kindness and love for unity, I decided to help people that I thought I can reason with, but it didn't work. I was innocent in all this, but I was dragged into worthless things. Through this situation, I learnt that not everyone is to be helped.

People who have pride in them, will never accept they were wrong, and they never apologise. This kind of characteristic in a servant of God is a turn-off, therefore we need to change and stop provoking or dragging innocent servants of God into mix-ups caused by you and not them.

I share this part of my reality, to show you how to deal with different kinds of people in or outside of ministry, without arguing or holding a grudge on them. In addition, my intentions were pure throughout hence, I don't feel guilty whilst sharing this. I ensured I apologised for any way I must have wronged her in the beginning or at the end of our conversation. After doing this, I felt so much peace within me, despite the hurtful things she said against me. In all this, I've learnt my lesson, especially when sensing the spirits operating behind people and even myself. I never knew things will escalate, the way it did.

If you find yourself in similar situations as a leader, where a friend or church member disrespects, degrades or accuses you, forgive and pray for that person. If you have something to say to them, do so in a calm manner or respond simply, "Thank you for your message, God bless you", by doing this, they will understand consciously that you're not happy about what they said against you, but you're choosing peace. At times, they also need to know that you were hurt, do this by distancing from them but don't hold a grudge against them. Pray to God to have mercy on them for they don't know what they are doing. Moreover, know how to live with such people and don't allow people to dine with your enemies and with you at the same time. Instead, leave them, if they don't want to change for your own peace.

# 17

## A HEART OF FORGIVENESS

In Luke 23:34, Jesus said, "Father, forgive them, for they do not know what they do. And they divided His garments and cast lots". Having a heart of forgiveness allows you to trample on snakes, scorpions and whatever that was holding you back in bondage. I went through a very difficult time in my life where I had to forgive people who bullied and destroyed my life in the past but thank God for healing and restoring me.

I had to find a reason why I should forgive these people that hurt and plotted against and took advantage of me, simply because Jesus died for our sins, he forgives us daily, so why can't I forgive others? To be honest it was very hard, as I spent all my teen years and childhood crying and wondering what I 've done to these people for this maltreatment and hate? So, I asked the Holy Spirit to work in and help me to forgive others and He did just that. Many at times we refuse to forgive others and forget that God forgives our sins daily or even every seconds. Matthew 6:14 says, "For if you forgive other people when they sin against you, your heavenly Father will also forgive you". I hear a lot of Christians pray and say, 'Lord forgive my enemies for all they've done to me", if they had the opportunity to release their enemies out of their hearts.

Know that, you are not actually releasing your enemies out of your heart if you're praying like this because it's your responsibility to forgive others, then God will forgive you just as you have forgiven others. This is how I used to pray when it came to prayers of repentance and confessions. But one day my Pastor Dr Leon taught us that we need to refrain from that kind of prayers and instead start to pray like this, "Lord I forgive my enemies for all they've done to me", if you can, do call out their names and name all the things, they've made you go through because it really helps in reviving the authenticity in you about the pains caused in the past or present. We need to get into the habit of doing this because God will not do it for you. This is for your own deliverance and freedom. Dr Juanita Bynum said, "Some things that happened, it was just not for me, that was their trouble and I forgive them……. For me not to forgive you, is me holding and carrying you around tomorrow in my brain. Now, so you become not just a distraction but an interruption to what I'm trying to accomplish". This is how unforgiveness effects our everyday lives.

When you don't forgive your enemies, you are building grudges, then hate, revenge and that's where the danger comes in because you will have no room to forgive them. Let me say this again, if you get to the point of holding grudges, vengeance, and hatred against your enemies, that's dangerous. It is dangerous for you and not for your enemies because they are already in trouble due to the pains, they've caused you. Now, when you don't remove the grudge, hate or vengeance in you, it means you are putting yourself into the trouble they're supposed to continue facing, instead of coming out of it, liberating yourself by forgiving them but you don't want to do that. Their troubles can discontinue if they confess and ask forgiveness before you and God.

When you do this, it means you are freely, deliberately, handing yourself into your enemies, when God wants you out. You are indirectly partaking and forcing yourself to experience the trouble they are going through because of hurting you. You are basically going to partake in the lack of sleep, the fear, the guilt, they currently facing. So, in other words, you're telling yourself this," okay, I want to experience their trouble too, I want to join you, I want to join their club too, I want to enjoy your trouble, the punishment you're facing because of hurting me, I want to partake in it too, I want to endure the pain you are enduring for hurting me, I want to also partake in their sin too, since I simply don't want to forgive you". A person who is mature enough, will not have this mentality.

You must know that God punishes the wicked, the sinners and those who are hurting you. Proverbs 11:21 says, "Be sure of this: The wicked will not go unpunished, but those who are righteous will go free". For example, imagine someone who has stolen your last hard-earned money and you are crying to God in prayer, "God vindicate me, punish the one who's stolen my hard-earned money, I've sweat to achieve this amount." Then God hears your prayers and trouble befalls them. Your cry has caused God to punish them through joblessness and making the money useless in their hands and causing them not to use it for anything good. But you are trying to tell God that he made a mistake in punishing them by you not forgiving them and deliberately partaking in their sin. Understand that God can never be wrong in what he does. This is the wrong way to use your power, authority, and dominion because you are losing the opportunity of a lifetime to make things right.

However, God still wants you to forgive them despite the punishment he has released onto them. If you don't forgive them, you will not go forward but backwards, while watching them going forward. You must do the needful, so you will not look stupid or crazy because of immaturity. If you didn't understand it this way before, do take this revelation into consideration now.

There was a day, in which, I cried so much like a baby in the presence of God just asking for God's mercy upon my accusers. This happened in a retreat that my good friend organised. God also led me to share this part of my testimony and how important it is to forgive others. I kept hearing the Holy Spirit say to me, "THE HEART OF FORGIVENESS", something that I've never heard in my life and I couldn't control the way I was feeling but it was so peaceful and convicting. I asked the Holy Spirit to explain what he meant. So, He said, people need to learn to have a heart that doesn't bear grudges and can easily look beyond people's mistakes and forgive, otherwise you will be hindering your own life from progressing and you wonder and see that the same people who you say, "Over my dead body, I can never forgive them" are going forward, whilst you're stuck in one place and struggling. When this happens, it means your accusers have dominated you. On that day I cried so much; in fact, I groaned for a good five minutes on the amount of time I refused to forgive these people. At that moment, it was as if my life was flashed in front my me and made me reflect. I was glad that I made the decision to let and let God revenge for me.

The people present, were amazed, touched, inspired, and convinced to do the same. Some were even telling their testimonies regarding what I shared and agreed with me on the topic. I really give God glory for touching their souls that day. It was not just a one-day thing but a whole process, I had to go through deliverance, confession, and forgiveness. I couldn't allow my enemies to keep dominating me, so I had to let them go out of my heart, so I can serve God freely, without any grudges or thoughts of revenge. In Luke 20:20 it says, "Keeping a close watch on him, they sent spies, who pretended to be sincere. They hoped to catch Jesus in something he said, so that they might hand him over to the power and authority of the governor". I had so many people who pretended to care for me, not knowing that they were sent to spy on me. Some of these people that maltreated and abused me were in my childhood church. As church leaders and humans in general, it is very crucial to have a heart of forgiveness, be quick to forgive your church members, pray for them and move on to other things. When you forgive, you do it for yourself and not for them. Servants of God, if you don't have a heart of forgiveness, you will give up easily on the work of God. In all this, I've learnt to grab this part of a lifetime opportunity for all, to forgive but not to be a fool. The Lord allowed me to win the battle, as my enemies confessed of their Witcraft and how they master minded evil so people can hate me and mess around with my reputation. The shocking of them all is that one of them was found mad and still mad till now, after he confessed that they were the cause of all the attacks I and my husband experienced. After, I forgave them in the secret, and forgave them all in public when I was invited for an interview. The Lord Jesus vindicated us and has started to render justice unto us.

This is where humility comes in, with forgiveness because if you can't humble yourself, you will never see change. Humility is also doing for others and that's another right way to take dominion. Humility allows people to see the grateful heart you have whether people praise you or not. Any time, humility occurs when people praise you, through this, others stay humble, but others take the opportunity to be prideful. Now, being proud in such case, indicates a bad way of dominion because a prideful individual will always be ungrateful, will dominate others negatively and will not listen or value others. You can boast in the Lord. God says in James 4:6 But He gives more grace. Therefore, He says: "God resists the proud, but gives grace to the humble."

# 18

# THE SIGNIFICANCE & BENEFITS OF PURITY

The Bible says, "Blessed are the pure in heart, for they shall see God" (Matthew 5:8).

Anyone has an opportunity of a lifetime to live in purity because it's not impossible but possible. Impurity is more popular than purity in this world. People love impurity than purity and this is an influence of the devil. Many people, especially Christians are struggling with this mentality of a *dirty mindset*. Impurity has dominated and overpowered people, due to lack of a prayer life and disobedience to God. So, when purity is mentioned, many get agitated and feel uncomfortable or condemned. Purity affects every areas of our lives and not just our sexualities. Purity is like is your identity. This eternal life is only possible by getting forgiveness of sins through faith in Jesus Christ. That's how powerful it is; therefore, God requires us to practice it in all aspects of our lives. It's something that will be eternal in our lives and it refers to heaven. Purity also means transparency and it tells people who you are and what you do, without saying a word. We need to understand that purity originates from the outcome of knowing and accepting that Jesus Christ gave his life and died for us to deliver us from impurities.

You can learn how-to live-in purity, as the bible teaches us on It, but you must make yourself available to learn and practice it. This means to protect yourself from negativity and from sin, so basically having the freedom from contaminations. In Ezekiel 44:23 Moreover, they shall teach My people the difference between the holy and the profane and cause them to discern between the unclean and the clean". A holy act glorifies God, but profane acts glorify the devil, the father of lies.

When you are clean, it gives you the boldness to dominate because cleanness is close to God, for He is holy. Living a life of purity allows us to pursue holiness and sanctification. There's a phrase that I hear a lot, "Cleanness is close to Godliness". The unclean with not be able to enter heaven, because our God is pure and never dwells in a dirty temple. This refers to spiritual and physical cleanness wherever we go. I know it can be very hard to maintain this but there's an opportunity of a lifetime for all. Meaning, any little time you have, take it and clean yourself spiritually and physically. In Leviticus 14:57, it says, "To teach when they are unclean and when they are clean. This is the law of leprosy". So, when we don't live a life of purity, we carry spiritual leprosy and pass them on to others. It's important I speak on this because many of us are struggling with it, in so many ways.

However, this doesn't mean I'm judging anyone or trying to be perfect. Many people can't maintain a life of purity, even when married, the devil is really after our purities. That's why we shouldn't play jokes with our purity status. I call it a status because, it's something we can have for a lifetime and can surely be maintained, despite the challenges. It's like a position you have been given in the society, and you are trusted to work hard to keep it.

Purity is a weapon for us to maintain as Christians, but the devil is after it continuously, so he can destroy us. He uses more of sexual sin to kill our life of purity. This includes sexual immorality, incest, adultery, fornication, masturbation, pornography, homosexuality, and other sinful acts. These evil acts are the opposite of purity, which is impure frequently, our minds are easily polluted by negativity and impurity through the TV, our environments, and surroundings.

This can have permanent implications in our lives, that could be a struggle to overcome. That's why It is important to be very careful and vigilant around others. Despite all, there are many benefits when you live in purity, which is peacefulness when the devil wants to frustrate you in living a life of impurity. You will gain a lot of respect and honour when you know how-to live-in purity. Living in purity will automatically show you the way to treat others with purity by not having impure thoughts against them. You will understand and refrain from treating people bad, by using impurity actions, including rape because you will know how important one soul to God is. Living a life of purity is also considered as a consecration and it helps build your relationship with God, by working together with the Holy Spirit, as a ransomed child of God. Purity is also a state of the mind and taking care of your mental health, emotional and physically health.

For example, if the doctors give you an instruction to keep an area of your life clean, you will obey. So, it's the same thing with purity, this is also a part of selfcare. Living in purity will birth integrity and that burning desire to advocate about it, even if people laugh at you. We live in a world full of anti-Christ's, where impurity is promoted left, right and centre, especially to younger people. When you live in purity, you will never attract gigolotic men", as I love to refer to men who sleeps with and feeds from women. When you live in purity, you will smell good both spiritually and physically. When you live in purity, the devil has a hard time in destroying you. It will be very difficult for him to win you over, through the fall of temptation because you understand, not just that but you are living it. The devil hates it when we practice the word of God. This shows you are physically and spiritually disciplined. People like David who were not stable in their life of purity, always faced the consequences. But the good thing about David is that he knew how to amend his ways. It is very important to ask God to help you live a life of purity and make it your routine, even if a man or women comes your way.

That man or women needs to know and respect your routine as a child of God. A routine is something that you do and keep. So, let purity stick on you like a super glue or magnet. Through purity, your actions affirm what Is right, it makes you live transparently. Purity also leads you to please God, love others and to remain humble. There are many benefits of purity which includes preferment, caution, discernment, and good choices as you work to avoid corruption in your thoughts. It will support you in good health, a long life and builds satisfaction and peace within. Purity will reveal the culpabilities in your life and branches you toward godliness, respecting the principles God gave you. Purity motivates you to avoid stumbling blocks and helps you live free of guilt and regret. Furthermore, purity nurtures a community of loving people and it dominates your relationships with others, with the opposite genders. Purity will turn you into a role model for others to follow. You can also pursue purity through a solid prayer life, perseverance, setting boundaries, and believing in yourself and God. But don't allow your purity to make you proud or to look down on others, remain humble.

# 19

## HOLINESS

Living a life of holiness is not the act of wearing vail over your head and remaining silent. But living a holy life is the act of pleasing God and respecting yourself. Imagine, if you were asked to marry a prostitute or a homosexual person as a Christian, you would refuse because they are committing acts of impurity. With a normal person, some may agree to be in a relationship with these kinds of people, but a Christian shouldn't be okay with it, unless it's the will of God.

The reason I say this is because I watched a United Kingdom reality show about relationships, a woman was not comfortable with dating a gay person but I'm not too sure if she was a believer of Christ or not. But she made her point clear, and the man also made it clear that he will remain gay, and nothing can change that, not even a female. So, as a Christian is very important to live a life sold to God, so that even the person you marry will see and agree to that. During my quite time, God ministered to me by telling my spirit that the celebrities, we see today have their lives sold out to the world. They are busy entertaining our screens by doing what doesn't glorify God and pleasing the world. They have become the world's puppets through the screens by dominating us negatively and they are very busy with it. Therefore, in the same way, we should be sold out to God in His presence, so that we can win souls to Him. Don't be too busy to do the things of God, that you only prioritise your children, home, marriage, and jobs. This means our entire lives must be given to God, entertaining the right things and for the right reasons. So even when we are on stage, ensure it's for the glory of God. Allowing your life to be sold out to God is deciding to be busy for God and making impact in holiness. This is another way of practicing positive power, authority, and dominion. The bible says in Matthew 6:33 But seek first his kingdom and his righteousness, and all these things will be given to you as well. This implies that we should follow a life of holiness, doing things that glorifies God. When you live a holy life, it causes people to respect, honour and consider you. People won't even dare to disrespect you because they see how you respect and carry yourself. Now, this is called authentic dominance because you are doing things right and people will have no choice than to be impacted. This implies that your positive way of living has allowed you to take dominion. According to the Christian bible, people who practice homosexuality are committing an abomination. This is a negative way of dominance, as it doesn't please God. In Leviticus 20:13 it says, "'If a man has sexual relations with a man as one does with a woman, both have done what is detestable. They are to be put to death; their blood will be on their own heads.

Now, God will not only punish the man but also the woman who practices this because they are dominating others negatively through a sinful lifestyle. I am not saying this to condemn such people but to speak the truth that is facts from the bible that all Christians should be aware of, as God does not rejoice in the death of a sinner, but he wants the sinner to repent, and they will be saved. Jesus Loves everyone but he detests the sin we commit, as it destroys our soul and makes us lose the power, he's given to us to dominate over everything.

As it's declared in Genesis 1:26-28 Then God said, "Let us make man in our image, after our likeness. And let them have dominion over the fish of the sea and over the birds of the heavens and over the livestock and over all the earth and over every creeping thing that creeps on the earth." So, God created man in his own image". If you still don't know, I need you to understand that it's a great privilege and honour to be given this opportunity. I mean, this is an opportunity of a lifetime for all, we can just believe in Jesus. God creates humans and gives them the care for everything else. By God giving humans dominion over the land and animals, He's giving humanity the right to govern and have power over all other living beings.

You must know that taking dominion is a big responsibility of its own and that means, you don't play jokes with it, as it involves not only you, but other hearts too. Taking dominion, is the idea of taking charge, serving, building, motivating, speaking, thinking out loud and being bold within and in the outward. You need to understand that God wants not just to give you opportunities to be blessed by, but also to be a blessing to others. You just need to believe in his timing, then you will declare that in a room full of opportunities, your name will be mentioned. Living a holiness lifestyle will help you achieve positive dominion.

This also means, you must take charge, dominion over your problems, setbacks, trials, persecutions, and tribulation. No one else will do it for you unless you do it yourself. This means you need to have spiritual authority which is given to you by God. Living in holiness will make you realise that kingdom authority is not autocratic. Being mindful that kingdom dominion is to rule and to be in charge. In addition, kingdom dominion is the ability to command and expect a fulfilment immediately or as a process. Therefore, you must take charge and command your body and mind to living in holiness by the power of the Holy Spirit.

Dominion is like taking personal convictions, if you are not convicted, you will never be able to dominate. To take dominion means you know who you are, your identity and what you stand for and what you represent. Whatever you choose to dominate is who you are, so choose wisely the things you choose to dominate. To dominate also means influence because people will listen to your instructions and principles when you carry dominion. The Christian bible also says in Leviticus 18:22 "do not have sexual relations with a man as one does with a woman; that is detestable. So, a person who really fears God, lives a holy life and is in their right senses, why would they be very comfortable in such a union? You can't dominate positively if you get yourself in such union because it's sinful and cause death. Each time we sin, we die spiritually but if we call on the blood of Jesus to dominate in us and cleanse us, we become pure and will be resurrected.

However, God says in Romans 6:14 For sin will have no dominion over you, since you are not under law but under grace. In addition, we can't be equally yoked with people who don't have the same conviction as us, not to run away from them but not to do what they do. As the bible declares in 2 Corinthians 6:14 "Don't team up with those who are unbelievers. How can righteousness be a partner with wickedness? How can light live with darkness? I mentioned a similar example as the above scripture about relationships. You see, I love the fact that the New Living Translation version of this scripture uses the word 'team up' to clearly describe what God wants us to understand.

The person you get involved with can determine your destiny and purpose. It will determine whether you will have the capacity to dominate what is coming ahead of you or not. Many people have no ability to take dominion of their destiny, purpose or anything crucial in their lives because you've teamed up with the wrong people. This is caused by lack of knowledge and understanding. In the past, my life was a mess because I teamed up with the wrong people out of loneliness, lack of knowledge and understanding, but now my life is a message because I team up with the right people for the right reasons. In addition, I live holy life by the grace of God. Once you sort these two out, in terms of dominion, you are halfway to be "good to go" in different areas of life.

When you team up with the wrong crowd, you become stuck and delayed. You can only dominate effectively with the right people. In my past life, I teamed up with the wrong people and wrong relationships. I got delayed and limited from doing good and walking in holiness. This nearly costed my life but thank God for His saving grace upon my life. I can now say that, I've now taken dominion over my destiny and purpose because I'm living in it. So, I ask "are you living in your destiny and purpose to take the right dominion?

God didn't create Adam and Adam or Eve and Eve, but he created Adam and Eve for a positive purpose. This implies that, gay and lesbianism is not to be practiced in Christianity. Therefore, we should do what God requires of us in the bible and not our own will. When you allow the will of God to prevail, it means you will indeed dominate and have a great influence on people. The dominion God gave us was not to harm people but to serve God's people with it. But When we use it wrongly, trouble comes.

# 20

## A Grateful Heart

An individual who has a grateful heart has the opportunity of a lifetime, to dominate correctly. Such individuals, God is always pleased with. This way God can see that you are using the dominion, power, and authority he gave you for his benefit. An ungrateful heart is useless before God because you care nothing about Him but yourself. If you want to continue progressing, a grateful heart will take you to where you want to be and sometimes places you have never thought of. Just think about the amount of people who lack the very things you have now, they wish to have it too, but they don't. Think of those who want to enjoy the cold and soothing super malt, Lucozade, Fanta, clean water or even the cocoa you are enjoying but they cannot. However, you have all this in your possession, some of which you don't even pay for, yet you are taking dominion, power, and authority over it in a wrong way, by taking advantage of it and not being grateful to God. When you look at what God has done for you, you should worship his name. You were complaining about the situation of your childlessness, financial situation, health issues, marriage, house, education issues and lack of employment. But the Lord has remembered you after all those sufferings, so the least you can do is to thank God, serve him and give him your undivided attention. This is how to take dominion, power, and authority in the right way. This is you returning the gratitude and a grateful heart to God.

It is also important to have a heart of worship to God because it shows that you are grateful. Being grateful to people God sent to be your destiny helpers, shows that you are dominating pride and ungratefulness. This means that you are not allowing your blessing to dominate you, but you are taking dominion over it by never forgetting God. Many people have allowed their money, houses, cars, relationships, alcohol, friends, beauty, makeup, appearance, dominate them.

This has led many to lose their power and authority over what God has created, for us to dominate. In addition, lots of people have allowed anger, hate, masturbation, pornography, grudges, and revenge dominate them because they still allow their flesh to operate against the will of God. That's why it's crucial to have a prayer life and train your body to obey what your spirit wants to do for God. Our flesh can lead us to serious troubles if we allow it to dominate and overpower us. That's why God says,"Then he returned to his disciples and found them sleeping. "Couldn't you men keep watch with me for one hour?" he asked Peter. "Watch and pray so that you will not fall into temptation. The spirit is willing, but the flesh is weak" Matthew 26:40-43. I love the fact that God emphasises on our spirits being awake because he understands how dangerous our flesh can be towards our spirits. Dominate your body because it is unwilling to do the things of God but of the world. When you do this, you are shaming the devil.

When you allow material things dominate you, your spirit sleeps and you can easily fall into temptation. Being awake in the spirit means to be vigilant, focus and not distracted by things around you. To watch and pray is something God needs us to do so we can be awake spiritually to pray, fast and worship God. I remember being very sick, I couldn't move or get up from the hospital bed, but I was able to open my mouth to pray and worship God, despite the pain.

The reason is because my spirit was awake and before my sickness I was already watching and praying. I didn't allow food or whatever I had physically and neither my situation dominate me from remaining in God's presence. When an individual cannot get their physical body to do this, it means their spiritual life is dead, it needs resurrecting. Your weakness is what destroys your spirit, and the impact is seen in your physical body. An example of this, is when you are trying to stop a bad habit, such as overthinking or an eating disorder, but you are struggling. Then you become moody, frustrated, and disturbed. At that point, your body becomes uneased, and your spirit becomes uncomfortable until you overcome your weaknesses. To dominate your weakness, you need to constantly pray and never stop. The more you pray, the more opportunity you will have to activate the power and authority that God put in you, to dominate over anything that disturbs your peace.

During Wife Let's Pray (Woman's Department at MPC Ministries) Prophetic prayer services that happens every Wednesdays on zoom. I had a wonderful time in the presence of God with the ladies, as the Holy Spirit led us into worshipping God. The Holy Spirit taught us in depth about the importance of being grateful in life. We ended up flowing in the prophetic and filled with testimonies that inspired us all. There's a prophetic song God gave me in 2020, that the Holy Spirit led me to share with the ladies on that day, which is called 'I'm grateful'. I had to emphasize on what a grateful heart can bring to our lives.

God wanted to remind us on reflection and understand the importance of all that we possess in our lives currently. There's power, dominion, authority inside a grateful heart. One of the ladies testified that God gave her husband a job in one the best hotels in Vienna and this was one of the prayer requests she brought in, so we can pray for her in Wife Let's Pray. The jobless issue was one of the things that caused arguments between her and her husband. But through prayer God answered her, at the exact moment when I prophesied that it was a month of good news. I asked each of them to sing the chorus of the grateful song I composed, and she did after testifying. There were so many testimonies from my mentees.

My heart was filled with joy, when I heard each of their testimonies about what they are grateful for. All this is to show you that, we, as Wife Let's Pray ladies international have decided to take dominion, power, and authority over our problems through praying and worshipping God. In this, God answered us and, to show our gratitude, we each testified about God's wonders in our marriages and lives.

God needs us to pray without ceasing, this helps to be in alignment with the will of God for us, no matter what the devil tries to do. God mentions it in 1 Thessalonians 5:17, "Pray without ceasing." Your persistence, dedication, perseverance, discipline, and consistency will determine how you dominate your trials in the present and future. Gratefulness goes along with faithfulness because you cannot receive unless you believe before seeing it. If you have faith, you have a lifetime opportunity, which others can enquire of too. To faith it in all, you need to dominate and allow God to lead you. A person who has the power to dominate must also carry faith in them as part of the criteria, otherwise you will not be able to operate positively and effectively. When you have faith and remain grateful to God, the creator, it triggers him to continue blessing you.

Prayer point: *Heavenly father, teach me how to maintain a grateful heart towards you, equip and strengthen me to pray without ceasing. Help me to have a heart of worship towards you, so that I will never be ungrateful in Jesus's name. Amen.*

# 21

## THE ISSUE OF HUMANITY

*"Do not take advantage of other but fear your God. I am the Lord your God."* Leviticus 25:17

Here, God has given the Israelites laws and things to do in the year of Jubilee, through his servant Moses. He warned them, in other words, no one should look down on or degrade anyone. This was a decree God made so that those who follow it will live safely in the land. Taking advantage of others, makes you weak and shows that you're insecure about yourself. This is dangerous because when someone understands your negative agenda against them, it will be catastrophic. Taking advantage of others is also seen as a negative act of dominion on innocent people. I've seen many rich people and servants of God take advantage of the poor and the less privileged. Some of them do this by yelling at them, throwing food on them by purpose, beating them up, bribing and threatening them just because they are begging for food or need financial assistance.

I saw a similar situation in a video on Instagram, where a well-known Pastor in Africa was aggressively shouting on top of his voice, at a poor woman in front of the pulpit, who needed his help in church. He asked the woman the amount of money she needed, but she couldn't talk due to breathlessness and tiredness and the food basket load she carried in her head. After, he pushed her back brutally, she nearly fell on the floor. Watching that video really destroyed my mood for the whole day, I was so angry to see a man of great impact maltreat a vulnerable woman. I hate seeing women being abused or anyone in general, as I know the pain of being abused. I believe in human rights and women rights, so I will point out anything that goes against it. People that take advantage of others exhibit the act of manipulation and control; they just can't mind their own business. They are always opening their eyes to find out what's not working in your life, so they use it against you and get an opportunity to mock you, whilst pretending to help.

This kind of demonic domination is very sad to comprehend but I've understood that people are not always what they present themselves to be, as appearance can deceive. The most category of people in the world that are taken advantage of is homeless people, orphans, widows, young children, and those with less or no educational background. When a person has the fear of God in them, they will never allow themselves to mistreat or take advantage of God's people. As humanity, we cannot live safely or at peace in the land if we keep on looking down on others. It is very costly to use people simply because you have power, authority, and dominion over them. Even if you have all this opportunity in your possession, it's humanly wise to use them correctly in empowering and not disgracing yourself by taking advantage of others.

The story of David in the bible is one that shows how much he was taken advantage of by his family and others. People saw David as a poor shepherd and a little boy who had nothing to offer. King Saul and his brothers tried to take advantage of him, but God saw him as a mighty king. When we look at Esther in the bible, she was an orphan, unvalued degraded but she became a queen and a hope to her nation. When others saw Sarah as a barren woman, God saw a mother of nations. God gave them the opportunity to dominate their mortifying situations in the right way. I encourage you now, that even if people pretend to not see you by taking advantage of you or refuse to extend the humanity token to you, remember that God sees you and your time will come. If we look in the Bible, those who tried or took advantage of others, God never let them go unpunished and he can still do that to anyone exhibiting this kind of negative domination. People who take advantage of others are nothing but bullies that need serious deliverance, else it will destroy even their next generation.

Another situation that's taking advantage of many, is the covid-19 virus. Lots of people have lost their lives and career jobs due to irresponsible and disobedient humans, who refused to isolate or wear their mask when it was compulsory. People have become more selfish then ever and not thinking about the vulnerable. Many have also lost their jobs, business, and companies due to the economic crises and the spread of the Covid-19 virus. Several people in their families are suffering in this season because people are taking advantage of others, due to no employment.

On the other hand, those who are encouraged, determined, motivated would pursue or look for other means to survive, by working at home, even when children are around. But there's a way for you to maintain your life financially, spiritually, and physically during the pandemic of Covid-19. You can do this by discovering other talents and gifts that is stored in you, which others don't have. Even if, others have done what you are planning to do already, as a way of surviving. You can still do it your way and be different. Build and revive those talents hidden in you, so that you will still have something going on. This way, people will refrain and think twice before taking advantage of you. Know the value of your hustle and talent so people will respect your brand and career, despite the pandemic. The moment you put your talents and gifts into use, it shows that you are working hard to practice positive domination, power, and authority for the glory of God. Don't look at yourself according to other people. Learn to discover you and don't be a copy but an original successor.

I've always had a question for people that take advantage of others, so just hear me out. How do you feel? what goes on in your mind? do you think you will live forever? what if your loved ones or blood related were taken advantage of what will you do? will you be happy?

So, think about these questions very well, if you see yourself reflecting and choosing to amend your ways, then this is the right way to dominate. Making the right decision will show that you've valued the power, dominion and authority given to you. It means you have dominated the evil spirit that dwelled in you to take advantage of others. Allow others to enter jubilation, even with the little they have whilst in your care. Help them whenever there's an opportunity but don't degrade them, as they are humans like you. Have the kind of dominating spirit of peace, joy and happiness that allows people to feel good about themselves, even when they don't have much.

Let the power, authority, and dominion of God that you possess, make others feel welcomed, worthy, wanted, cared for, listened to and valued, especially in their lowest moments. Let the power, dominion and authority living in you bring hope to the hopeless. When you know how to dominate in the right way, it will make the unbelievers believe and those who lost faith in God will rebuild it. It all depends on how we treat people, even if we are being misunderstood by others. This is what proves that you have positive dominion, power, and authority in you that others can benefit from.

People who have discernment, will know whether you are dominating correctly or not, if you are, it will attract others to approach you. But if you are the kind of person that dominates in a wrong way, people will distance from you because you are being a user and taking advantage of others. Also, it doesn't mean if you are older than the individual who is respecting you, that you should take advantage of them, forgetting that they could be wiser then you. Therefore, it is important for us to fear the Lord our God and refrain from mistreating and taking advantage of others. If not, you will lose friends and opportunity of a lifetime, and then lose yourself in the process.

Prayer point: *Lord help me to stop taking advantage of the people you created. Give me a heart for humanity, so I can use the power, dominion, and authority you have given to me as tools of blessings and not manipulations in Jesus's name, Amen.*

# 22

# THE MYSTERY OF BEING HALF DEAD (LUKE 10:30)

The mystery of being half dead is taken lightly by many, but it is the opposite of the essence of life at its fullest. Living a half dead life is dangerous because your spiritual and physical organs will not function in its full potential. It is dangerous to be in this situation because things will not work for you. It causes instability, stagnation, delay, depression, stroke, failure, and limitations.

Who or what has left you dead in this life? There's no way that you can take dominion If you are half dead. Is it the man, the woman, the anxiety, or nightmare etc. A half dead life is a half dead destiny, purpose, projects, goals, visions, and ambitions. A person who is half dead, is not useful as much as they were, when fully alive. Be aware that spiritual death is worse than physical death because it is our body that dies but our souls remain. So, you can lose your body but if your soul is in Christ Jesus, you are saved and will not die but have eternal life. It is our sins that causes death in us, so we may be alive physically but spiritually half dead or even dead completely.

This leads us to Romans 6:23 where Paul writes that the rewards or "wages" of our sin and unrighteousness is always "death." The word sin means to "miss the spot" of God's desires (Romans 3:23), so any penalties that come along with falling short are deserved and appropriate. Our sinfulness naturally results in death and dying in three unique waves, such as emotionally, physically, and spiritually. Let's take all three into consideration.

God instructed Adam and Eve to eat from every tree in the Garden of Eden except the "tree of the knowledge of good and evil… for in the day that you eat of it you shall surely die" (Genesis 2:16-17). But when they ate from the forbidden tree and committed the first sins of humanity, it shows they died. When someone is half dead, it shows that they are in coma and needs to always be resuscitated to be fully awake. When someone is sick, they can't do their daily activities effectively because one part of the body is not regulating properly. You will be forced to do things that people tell you to do and you can't eat, drink, or wear what you want. You will be obliged to rely on other people to do things for you. Until you fully recover. An individual who is suffering from stroke are between life and death and most people escape from it and some don't. You will always depend on others, even to bath or feed, but the problem with this is that many people can take advantage of you and start doing things on purpose to hurt you.

Living a half dead life is living in bondage and slavery in your own body and surrounding. Living a half dead life, means you are unaware of the unknown and could be deceived a lot. In this situation, you can't really finish things you started at its appointed time, things will be delayed and limited. It's a whole mess and disaster to be in such situation. Others are going through this physically, but others are going through a half dead life spiritually. Now, I want to focus on the spiritual aspect of this because it's a mystery that needs to be unfolded. It's time to wake up from your spiritual coma and I command it to be so, with immediate effect in Jesus's name.

# 23

# REVELATION BEHIND SPIRITUAL & PHYSICAL NAKEDNESS

Spiritual nakedness is an indication of being unprotected and utterly exposed. So, who's left you naked? you can't take dominion if you're spiritually naked. Lots of people even have dreams where they find themselves, half naked or completely naked. This is very dangerous because it means the door of your life is open for spiritual rapists, demons, thieves, and bullies to enter. Even in the physical, no one will respect you as a decent person. They will think as if you're crazy and mental enough to expose yourself the way you do. If you are spiritually naked, know that it's not normal at all. It shows that there's something wrong; either you've been targeted to be attacked or you've physically done something that has stripped you off your clothes or spiritual mantels.

In Luke 10:30-37 In reply Jesus said: "A man was going down from Jerusalem to Jericho, when he was attacked by robbers. They stripped him of his clothes, beat him and went away, leaving him half dead. A priest happened to be going down the same road, and when he saw the man, he passed by on the other side. So too, a Levite, when he came to the place and saw him, passed by on the other side. But a Samaritan, as he traveled, came where the man was; and when he saw him, he took pity on him. He went to him and bandaged his wounds, pouring on oil and wine. Then he put the man on his own donkey, brought him to an inn and took care of him. The next day he took out two denarii and gave them to the innkeeper. 'Look after him,' he said, 'and when I return, I will reimburse you for any extra expense you may have. "Which of these three do you think was a neighbor to the man who fell into the hands of robbers?" The expert in the law replied, "The one who had mercy on him." Jesus told him, "Go and do likewise."

This scripture links with the mystery of being half dead, as these people destroyed him and left him in a horrible state, where he fought for his life. The cause of his physical nakedness and being left half dead, was an attack but he was innocent. Sometimes, people with no sense, will choose to attack others for no valid reasons and leave half dead and spiritually naked. Therefore, you must pray deeper, revive, and cover yourself in the blood of Jesus, so that you will remain on fire for Jesus. Your spiritual covering or exposure shows through your lifestyle or a pattern of things occurring in your life.

In Genesis 3, God had no choice than to kill an animal to cover Adam and Eve's nakedness, after realising that they ate the fruit from the forbidden tree. That's what caused there spiritual and physical nakedness. This is to show you that, after this happened it was not a good idea to be publicly naked, hence why we wear clothes. To be naked at home is fine, that's your space but when it comes to the public, it's not appropriate. I am aware that when dressing up, you will be naked because its common sense. However, we should cover their body for the glory of God in public. The way you physically carry yourself, is the result of how you carry yourself spiritually. If you don't respect your body, then demons won't respect it either. When you pray to God, you're spiritually covering and keeping yourself from spiritual nakedness. As a result, your physical body will adapt to how your spiritual being is leading it, you begin to know the difference between a covering and what's not covering.

Spiritual nakedness is an evidence that you have fallen short of the glory of God and your prayer life is on low battery. Sometimes, it could just be the stress of life and a negative mindset. There was a time in my life, I had a dream where I was being called a Prophetess by a

Pastor and was asked to do a closing prayer. But I told them, wait, my iPhone is on 1% low battery, let me charge it. During those days, I was going through a lot both spiritually and physically. As a result of that, I couldn't really pray like I used to. So, I would understand the reason for such dream. The devil was trying to strip me off my calling, but I stood in prayer and regained my power through prayer. When you have these kinds of dreams, it's God reminding you to recharge your spiritual battery; meaning to watch and pray.

Another example is when I had a dream that I was half naked and I didn't have slippers, but I prayed concerning it and claimed back my spiritual clothes and destroyed any source that's causing this problem. After praying, I never had that kind of dreams again. Many times, you would see these kinds of dreams through bad connections, dirty conversations with other people and other family attacks.

Maybe you're reading this now and you've realised that, ever since you met a certain friend, you haven't been praying, working, focusing, disciplined like you was before. This means that the person you encounter, is slowly stripping you off and leaving you spiritually naked, due to jealousy or has a mission to destroy you willingly. Your ministry, marriage, businesses, children, and home may also be spiritually naked, that's why things in those areas are not functioning.

This is an indication that you need to pray without ceasing because demonic forces are close to you. A lifetime opportunity here is knowing the cause of your physical or spiritual nakedness and measurements to take to rekindle your prayer life. Most problems in our lives are the cause of our spiritual nakedness. Spiritual nakedness can make one to act like a mad person because people will view you as weird and they will run away from you, as they will assume you are cursing them. Furthermore, people will choose to go naked to carry out an assignment, but that's usually a demonic one. However, there are some reasons why some people would go naked for a while, only if it is the will of God. As the Bible mentioned about a servant of God in this season.

Isaiah 20 says, "Under the orders of Emperor Sargon of Assyria, the commander-in-chief of the Assyrian army attacked the Philistine city of Ashdod. Three years earlier the LORD had told Isaiah son of Amoz to take off his sandals and the sackcloth he was wearing. He obeyed and went around naked and barefoot. When Ashdod was captured, the LORD said, "My servant Isaiah has been going around naked and barefoot for three years. This is a sign of what will happen to Egypt and Ethiopia. The emperor of Assyria will lead away naked the prisoners he captures from those two countries. Young and old, they will walk barefoot and naked, with their buttocks exposed, bringing shame on Egypt. Those who have put their trust in Ethiopia and have boasted about Egypt will be disillusioned, their hopes shattered. When that time comes, the people who live along the coast of Philistia will say, 'Look at what has happened to the people we relied on to protect us from the emperor of Assyria! How will we ever survive?'

Your appearance can also play a major role in the cause of your spiritual nakedness because you are seducing people by the way you present, dress and act. That means you are being a stumbling block to others and causing their eyes to sin and eventually become spiritually naked. A lot of Christians cannot stay in one church, they have many pastors. This shows they don't have a spiritual covering; they are spiritually naked. Also, you will notice that their lives are so unstable. You need to have a spiritual covering and ensuring that you are wearing the full armour of God.

Ephesians 6:11-18, "Put on the whole armour of God, that ye may be able to stand against the wiles of the devil. For we wrestle not against flesh and blood, but against principalities, against powers, against the rulers of the darkness of this world, against spiritual wickedness in high places. Wherefore take unto you the whole armour of God, that ye may be able to withstand in the evil day, and having done all, to stand. Stand therefore, having your loins girt about with truth, and having on the breastplate of righteousness; And your feet shod with the preparation of the gospel of peace; Above all, taking the shield of faith, wherewith ye shall be able to quench all the fiery darts of the wicked. And take the helmet of salvation, and the sword of the Spirit, which is the word of God."

Here, God has given us clear instructions on what to wear from top to toe, as a full armour of God. Wearing the full armour of God will protect you from spiritual nakedness and other attacks. This means, we must claim, confess it with power, dominion, authority regularly. When you do this, you are giving yourself a lifetime opportunity, that will bring you peace and purpose.

Prayer point: *Lord, send a good Samaritan, to help me. Father avenge for me, those who stole from me, those who beat me and went away. I put on the full armour of God. Strengthen me to take dominion by being a good Samaritan. Deliver me from any spiritual nakedness and spiritual death in Jesus's name. Be a good neighbour to my fellow sister or brother, instead of tearing each other's down. Jesus said, go and do likewise.* (Luke 10:30)

# 24

# THE TRUTH BEHIND DESTINY AND PURPOSE

Dominion plays a great part in your destiny and purpose. There are many things that are hidden behind destiny and purpose, especially when it comes to dominion, power, and authority. Most people don't tell you the truth on how sweaty, tired, confused, lonely you can become in the process and as you settle down in your purpose and destiny. If you are not a courageous, determined, motivated and resilient person than you can't dominate things that are trying to stop you from fulfilling your purpose and destiny. In life there's a thing called destiny helpers and many of us are struggling to find them because we are either, ignorant or refusing to accept unexpected help. There is also the spirit of, "Almost there but never there" in our lives, which needs to stop, otherwise we won't discover our destiny and purposes. We have a lifetime opportunity which is to live in our purposes and destinies but there are things blocking you from being lifted. This reminds of the story about the man who was begging at the temple gate called Beautiful Gate. In Acts 3:2-8, "Now a man who was lame from birth was being carried to the temple gate called Beautiful, where he was put every day to beg from those going into the temple courts. When he saw Peter and John about to enter, he asked them for money. Peter looked straight at him, as did John. Then Peter said, "Look at us!" So, the man gave them his attention, expecting to get something from them. Then Peter said, "Silver or gold I do not have, but what I do have I give you. In the name of Jesus Christ of Nazareth, walk." Taking him by the right hand, he helped him up, and instantly the man's feet and ankles became strong. He jumped to his feet and began to walk. Then he went with them into the temple courts, walking and jumping, and praising God.

This scripture has proven to me how useless it is when we expect too much from people. This is what I didn't like about the crippled man, you can't always expect things from people, and we need to look at God through his servants because in them is the I AM, who is Jesus Christ. This man has been crippled all his life and begged for help in at a temple gate called Beautiful Gate. Although the gate was called beautiful, it was still receiving broken people at the gate. The man gave them his attention, expecting to get something from them. One thing I've personally seen and loved from what Rev Lucy Natasha preached in terms of purpose and destiny, people expect the healing but not the, healer. We have become his poesy, a redesigned people that will fulfil the destiny he has given each of us, for we are joined to Jesus, the Anointed One. But people now expect the anointing but not the anointer, they expect the blessing but not the blessing. They want to live in their destiny and purposes, but they don't want God who is directs us to our destiny and purposes. Now, this mentality to me just doesn't make sense! because humans are just human, they can disappoint you at any given opportunity but when expect from God, you receive a lifetime opportunity for all. Before we were even born, he gave us our destiny; that we would fulfil the plan of God who always accomplishes every purpose and plan in his heart. Your purpose and destiny can be tied with someone else, that's why you see people getting married and walking together. If you know that you have a calling into your purpose and destiny, you've got be around those who carry the mantle, the wisdom, power, dominion, and authority about that field, so they can lift you.

Ephesians 2:10 For we are God's handiwork, created in Christ Jesus to do good works, which God prepared in advance for us to do. To step into your destiny and purpose, you need to accept preparation.

You need to be moulded, prepared, broken, amended, humbled in advance before you are released into your destiny. Your destiny and purpose are something that God has already programmed for you to be doing ln life, that's why you need to discover it and expect God to lead you to get there, through his servants and those he sends as your destiny helpers. Peter and John were sent as a destiny helper to the crippled man, but it was unfortunate that the crippled man was expecting something from them, instead of expecting from the God in them. Despite this, God still used them to help him up, this means they lifted him, and he received the power to walk. A lot of people lose the opportunity of being lifted into their destiny because they are surrounded by destiny helpers, but they are not ceasing the opportunity. You need to benefit from the good people surrounding you because in them at least one of them could be God-sent to be your destiny helper. Your situation should never stop you from fulfilling destiny or purpose because it never stops this crippled man. Hatred, bullying, pains, rejection shouldn't stop you from fulfilling destiny and purpose because other people are counting on your destiny and purpose, as in it could be their breakthrough.

If what you call "your destiny" is not giving glory to God and it's not leading you to doing good works, then it's not his purpose for you. Your purpose is meant to glorify God, the activities God called you to do is your destiny. Even before we were born, God planned our destiny and the good works we would do to fulfil it.

Living your best life is living in your purpose and destiny. Your destiny was never to be dressing half naked and posing on social media and calling yourself an influencer. Your destiny is more than that, deeper and beyond what you think it is. What are you exactly Influencing? What's your purpose? Your purpose and destiny are anything that glorifies God, but if it doesn't, then it's time to kiss it goodbye and never look back. Never doubt God's mighty power to work in you and accomplish all this. He will achieve substantially more than your greatest request, your most implausible dream, and surpass your wildest thoughts! He will top them all, for his astounding power always rejuvenates you.

# 25

## The Mystery of Blindness

A blind person is some one that cannot see and that's their default. But here's the thing about blindness that made me think. A blind person may not see but they can still do other things such as listening, smelling, writing, walking etc. This allows them to dominate, have power and take authority in their own unique way. The mystery is that people still pay attention to them, people still speak to them, people still consult them in many things, especially if they have academic skills. Blind people never allow their disabilities stop them from taking dominion, power, or authority. I've seen sports that are uniquely for disabled people, that includes the blind. Sports such as goalball, which is a three-a-side team game, developed for blind and partially sighted players but those who can fully see can play it too. There are also marathon runners such as Marla Runyan, she won more than one national championships. Hannah Russell who is young and has a visual impairment and swims in the Olympics. She came first in Paralympic titles (GOLD) Tokyo Paramedics. This, for me is inspiring because they are using their gifts and talents to contribute to the humanity in a positive way. Despite blindness being one's physical weakness, it doesn't stop them from being great. They broke the barrier and decided to use their disabilities to inspire others and it has indeed worked.

Even if they can't see, they still have great influence, impact and value. The mystery in blind people is the effort to ensure that they use their gifts and talents to communicate to the world. Some blind people do this through singing, rapping, writing, drawing, dancing, and doing many other things with other people's assistance. Lots of blind people are taken advantage of in this world and are fooled by many. When the blind does this, it means they've grabbed an opportunity of a lifetime for all, to dominate the world positively. As they use their gifts and talents, you will notice that people are drawn to them, many will be fascinated and get inspired. You will also realise that most blind people are very persistent, focused, determined, and confident of who they are. The blind use parts of their senses to survive, they can smell when someone is around them and can speak out when something is wrong. They don't always rely on their stick, as it could mislead them, but they rely more on their nose, ears, and mouth to dominate any negativity.

Bartimaeus in the bible is a perfect example of blindness because he was physically blind and never gave up, even though the crowd were preventing him to come near Jesus. But, in the end he encountered Jesus and he was healed. He knew that he had a mission to fulfil when he heard about Jesus. He's mission was to get to where Jesus was, so his life can be transformed. He was very determined, persistent, focused, loud, and confident that Jesus was there and located him. Bartimaeus sensed that it was his day of victory and healing, so he grabbed the opportunity. The blind cannot physically see but they can fix equipment's, give solutions to complex situations. So, this means that people with visual impairment are important to the society too, as their abilities allow them to contribute to the community through positive domination. You would probably wonder, how is this possible? Well, I will have you know that everything is possible to the one that believes.

For the bible says in Matthew 19:26, "And looking at them Jesus said to them, 'With people this is impossible, but with God all things are possible.'" The word possible simply means, it can happen if you make it happen. When you refuse to make it happen, it's impossible to see it happen. In this verse, we can understand that the blind allowed God to make everything else good in them to happen, despite their disability. Give an opportunity to yourself to see the impossibilities become possibilities because in you there's power, authority, and dominion.

This scripture describes that Jesus looked at them, this means he could see them spiritually because God is Spirit, he could also see them physically (When Jesus was in a human form). He knew their thoughts, intentions and their motives and responded to them accordingly. Now, the mystery is that if you can't see, it's difficult to know people's intentions, motives, and thoughts toward you. This happens in another way too, which is spiritual blindness, and many people suffer from this. Several Christians can physically see and don't require glasses but can't see spiritually and will need spiritual glasses. In addition, the non-ability of not seeing spiritually is more dangerous than physical blindness. When you are spiritually blind, you will not know how to lead your life because everything will be like a blind spot before you.

Being spiritually blind, will block you from discovering or exercising your gifts and talents. If you are spiritually blind, it means you are not watching and praying. If both of this seems to be the problem with you, try your best to resolve one of them or both when you can. Remember, a blind person cannot lead the blind, one must make more effort, so there will be a balance. In all this, we should never underestimate anyone, whether they are poor, have visual impairment, other disabilities, lonely or suffering. Know that there's an opportunity of a lifetime for all of us. Know that you are like an eagle, clothed with strength, power, authority and dominion. Remember, if you're still alive there is hope and hundreds of opportunities to grab and work on.

# 26

## A STEP FORWARD

Hebrews 4:16 "Let us then approach God's throne of grace with confidence, so that we may receive mercy and find grace to help us in our time of need". I need you to know and understand that the grace of God is sufficient for you and me. To take dominion, authority, and power, you need a positive mindset and a healthy mental attitude that would allow you get a lifetime opportunity. Remember one thing, you can't get the prize if you don't step forward, you've got to push to get to the throne. When you have confidence, fear has no place. Confidence means you need to take a step forward into glory, just like queen Esther in the bible. She took a bold step forward and she became a queen, despite her history of being an orphan. A throne is sacred and only one person can sit on it. The one who understands what they possess and can grab a positive opportunity that's approaching them is worthy to sit on the throne too.

The throne represents glory, power, authority, and dominion. Stop self-pitying, approach Jesus and He will redirect you to the right people and those right people will signpost you to relevant organisations. You've got to have something stored in you to approach God's throne and this should be your willingness to do. It's like going for a job interview and you haven't got your CV, how will they be sure you are suitable for the job? You need tangible evidence, apart from the word of your mouth. You need your CV to approach the throne. Your CV is your confidence, faith, hope, power, dominion, authority, wisdom, and the willingness to do. Your spiritual CV is having the Holy Spirit and a prayer life. Your physical CV is anything that you've obtained professionally, and it represents you, such as your education, career, hobbies, and interests. You can start building your Godly CV through your willingness to do. The woman with the issue of blood (Luke 8:43-48) took a step forward, approached Jesus boldly and she was healed. She gained confidence to approach God's throne of grace through Jesus Christ His son, that's why she saw a difference. Taking a step forward means you want change and now! It's an immediate move. A person with an open heart simply means, you accept your mistakes and consequences, but you decide to learn and to keep it moving, despite how horrible the world has treated you. Being willing to be helped, is what makes you have an open heart. Be open minded and stop isolating yourself at home doing nothing. Go out there and explore what God has for your purpose and destiny. Discover your hidden gifts, talents, and approach boldly into God's throne. Go out to the community and socialise, as there's plenty of good opportunities for you.

I hear mother's say (I say this too as a mother) "I'm only doing it for my children", the same confidence you have when you're trying your best to ensure that your child doesn't see how sad you are. The same confidence you have when you're trying to make your child happy, when they say "mummy, daddy I want bread" or "play with me... hug me". But at that moment you are not in the right frame of mind. On top of that, you are angry, moody, depressed, but deep down you want to do whatever it takes to also please your child. That's why you will have that confidence to say, "I'm doing this just for my child, I'm working because of my child".

So, have the same confidence to do better things and when you're approaching the Lord. Have that same confidence when you're entering the place of glory. Activate that same confidence to make a step forward and do what you must do for God's glory. I know it's going to be difficult but the same confidence you use to maintain your communication with your children or with others, use it to maintain and approach God's throne of grace, even if you are not happy, make a step forward to see what good is waiting for you ahead. Remember a closed mouth, is a closed destiny.

No one wants to be around someone who is lazy, complaining and doesn't want to move forward. If you have a friend who is full of courage and confidence, they will also influence you to obtain the courage and confidence too, whether you like it or not. If you choose to be around them, you will be obliged to take a step forward. Confidence and courage are like a disease, it's very infectious. I would rather have that kind of friend to infect me with confidence and courage than to remain empty with so many friends without that criteria.

You can't pour from an empty cup, that's why you need Jesus who is filled to withdraw you from the emptiness. For this to happen, you need to approach God's throne of grace with confidence so He can pour in you and reform you into a better and stronger person. I say this because I can very much relate to this when I look at my past. I was completely damaged mentally, spiritually, and physically. It like as if I was running mad at some point because I could no longer handle the problems. The bible says In Genesis1: 1-2 "In the beginning God created the heavens and the earth. Now the earth was formless and empty darkness was over the surface of the deep, and the spirit of God was hovering over the waters".

I was empty and without form, but God formed and filled my heart, soul, body, and spirit. My mind was failing me, but I found a man who renewed my mind, and his name is Jesus. Spiritually He got me aligned with my destiny and purpose at my breaking point of depression, anxiety, suicidal thoughts, fears, and panic attacks. All of this led me to seeking love from wrong the people, that I indulged in lesbianism, masturbation, and other sexual immorality activities. This is evil, so I had to denounce them and find an opportunity for deliverance and you know what? I got it! And I'm free from these negative dominion activities by the grace of God.

# PRAY WITH ME

*Heavenly Father, thank you for everything I've learnt in this book. Please give me the strength to take every good opportunity you give me, to pray, grow and work to be a better version of myself. Give me an eye like an eagle and revive in me your dominion, power, and authority so I can conquer the world. Help me to have a positive impact on others and show kindness all the time. Deliver me, o God from anything that doesn't glorify you. In Jesus name, Amen.*

# ACTIVITY: PAD THERAPY

Below is a self-confidence activity invented by myself, which I've named PAD Therapy. PAD stands for Power, Authority and Dominion. It's designed to promote positive mental health wellbeing. It is specially for mentally damaged individuals. This therapy is a lifetime opportunity for all, therefore its designed for all ages. Through PAD Therapy, I aim to help people gain back their confidence to grab positive opportunities that approaches them in life and not to stay in one place of sadness but to step forward. This will benefit you not just mentally but also emotionally, physically and spiritually.

Have a try:

1. Stand up, then breath in and out twice.

2. Take a step forward, then pause and close your eyes.

3. Reflect on how your life is going... what's stopping you from being confident?

4. Take a step forward from everything hindering you and denounce them 1 by 1 as you continue stepping forward.

For example:

* I take a step forward from depression

* I take a step forward from anxiety

* I take a step forward from laziness

* I take a step forward from discouragements

* I take a step forward from post traumatic disorder

* I take a step forward from negativity

* I take a step forward from limitations

* I take a step forward from betrayal

* THEN SMILE

What do you realise after doing this?

After this activity, you would realise that:

* You can do it

* You are not in the same spot as before

* Refusal of isolation, delay, limitations and stagnation

* Nothing is stopping you from moving forward anymore

* Constantly making a move from all things unhealthy.

* Which shows that you refuse to go backwards

* A chance to start again

* Willing to make a change

* A positive approach

* Relieved

* Recharged

* Stronger

* Peacefulness

* Hopefulness

* Encouraged

* Empowered

* Strengthened

This is an open heart kind of person who has decided to take the opportunity to dominate, regain their power and authority.

# The Author

Evangelist, referred often as woman of many talents and Mama Different. Born in Congo and based in United Kingdom. A mother, wife, a children's author, motivator, speaker, intercessor , advocating mental health, bullying and abuse. A business woman, songwriter, worshipper, Award winning inspirational leader and mentor by Maranatha Awards USA. Naomie Praise was ordained as an Evangelist in July 2021 and operates in the prophetic, healing and deliverance.